D0837101

The Hermitage

The Home of General Andrew Jackson
Seventh President of the United States

A HISTORY AND GUIDE

Published by

THE LADIES' HERMITAGE ASSOCIATION
JAMES E. ARNOLD, DIRECTOR, THE HERMITAGE
ROUTE 4, HERMITAGE, TENNESSEE

1967

CONTENTS

FRONT COVER © 1965 NATIONAL GEOGRAPHIC SOCIETY

Andrew Jackson's Hermitage

The Hermitage, with its "mansion house" and surrounding farm, was the home of Andrew Jackson, seventh President of the United States, Hero of the Battle of New Orleans and the greatest Tennessean in the history of the state.

Andrew Jackson was a national figure, generally recognized as one of the four greatest American Presidents. The Hermitage is a national shrine, preserved in his memory by The Ladies' Hermitage Association.

The people of Middle Tennessee and Davidson County, descendants of Jackson's friends and neighbors, have had a special love for the Hermitage and for the memory of Jackson. A farmer, lawyer, judge, soldier and statesman, he lived and farmed in the Hermitage community for more than half a century. With his wife Rachel he managed the farm, grew cotton, fed and clothed the slaves and brought up children (though not their own) in sickness and health, fair weather and foul, just as did other people in the community.

Andrew Jackson was a strong and determined man, ambitious and fearless. He made enemies both at home and on a national scale. But the friends and neighbors who loved him were many, and are a part of the story of his life. The spark of affection did not die. It is kept alive today by The Ladies' Hermitage Association, a group which has cherished the memory of Jackson for three-quarters of a century, and has preserved the Hermitage for the world.

The Hermitage, with its green fields and stately trees, the house and its furnishings, the garden and the tomb, is an expression of a man and his times, symbolizing an almost forgotten way of life. It reflects the character and taste of Andrew Jackson, and his love for his wife.

At various times during Jackson's life—though never since—the Hermitage was remodeled or changed in some way. In 1834, after a disastrous fire which spared only the west wing, it was rebuilt on the same foundations, with the same brick walls. The structure emerged as a "cobbled" house, rough-hewn, perhaps, but grand. It may lack some of the graceful beauty of other white-pillared Southern homes—it is not quite like any of them.

The Hermitage has its own distinct character, its own greatness, and its own style. And thus the house reflects the qualities of the man who built it, cultivated its fields and planted its trees. There was never another man like Jackson.

Andrew Jackson was of Scotch-Irish descent. He was born March 15, 1767, at the Waxhaw settlement in Lancaster County, South Carolina, near the North Carolina line, the son of Andrew and Elizabeth Hutchinson Jackson. His parents had come from Carrickfergus, in the north of Ireland, in 1765.

Andrew Jackson's father died before he was born, and upon his mother fell the burden of bringing up her three sons during the stormy and desolate years of the American Revolution. The Red Coat army came to the Waxhaw settlement, and as a stripling boy Andrew Jackson learned of the hardships of war. He learned, too, in that harsh struggle that took the lives of his mother and two brothers, to regard the British as implacable enemies. It was an enmity he never forgot, and he lived to repay their every blow.

Despite his tender years, Jackson actually took part in the conflict. At the age of 13 he fought with Continental troops against the British regulars at the Battle of Hanging Rock, Aug. 1, 1780— at about the same time the city of Nashville was born on the bluffs of the Cumberland. The next year, in an attempt to capture a body of British soldiers at Waxhaw church, Jackson was taken prisoner.

Ordered to black the boots of a British officer, Jackson, then 14, refused, and the officer struck him with a sabre. The blow inflicted wounds on Jackson's head and arm which he never forgot or forgave. One of Jackson's brothers was killed in the war, and the other died of smallpox. His mother died of a fever while nursing American prisoners held by the British.

Young Jackson was now the only surviving member of his immediate family. He attended several schools in the Waxhaw neighborhood. The extent of his formal schooling is not accurately known, but he was probably very well educated for his time and place. He even taught school for a while in the neighborhood. All his life he was to be an uncertain speller, and he could mispronounce words with unusual emphasis. He was, however, an effective writer who could move and inspire men with the urgency of his words.

An Irish grandfather died, leaving young Andrew an estate worth "three or four hundred pounds sterling," besides which he had inherited 200 acres of land. By this time, however, Andrew was very much interested in fast horses—even as a youth he was known as a fine judge of horse flesh—and such amusements as cock-fighting and cards also claimed his attention. A little later, his inheritance very much diminished, Andrew was in Salisbury, North Carolina, studying law.

Under Spruce McCay, and later under Col. John Stokes, Jackson studied law and so applied himself that by the time he was 20 he was licensed to practice law. Colonel Stokes was one of the most brilliant figures in the annals of the North Carolina bar. Having lost a hand in the Revolution he had it replaced with a silver knob, and at points of his courtroom speeches he would bring it down on the table, making it ring like a bell. Members of the Stokes family have been prominent lawyers in both Tennessee and North Carolina, and descendants are practicing law in Nashville today.

As a young lawyer Andrew Jackson looked west for opportunity. It was a land where fortunes could be made, or lost. In the fall of 1788 we find him riding across the mountains with Judge John McNairy, equipped with a mare, a rifle, two pistols and half a dozen law books. In October he arrived at Nashville on the Cumberland, a log cabin town surrounded by a buffalo fence, and began his duties as prosecuting attorney for the Western District of North Carolina, in the superior court presided over by Judge McNairy.

Andrew Jackson had now entered upon the stage which would shape his life. He worked hard, moved fast, made friends and some enemies. He boarded with the widow of pioneer John Donelson, and there began the series of events which foreshadowed trials and triumphs in the years ahead. The highlights of his career are filled with action and drama, and the final triumph of those virtues which he had from his mother, and which he never abandoned to the day of his death.

HIS MARRIAGE

Rachel Donelson Robards was the daughter of Col. John Donelson, one of the founders of Nashville. When Jackson came to live at the widow Donelson's home Rachel was there. She was a beautiful woman, and a female relative noted that she was "irresistible to men." After three years of marriage to Capt. Lewis Robards of Kentucky, she had been sent home from Harrodsburg by her husband, with an unsupported charge that she had been too friendly with a young attorney named Peyton Short. Robards' own mother sided with Rachel, believing her innocent. Robards vacillated and then returned to the Cumberland to reclaim his wife. She went back to him, but before long there was another quarrel— and this time the name Robards hurled at his wife was that of Andrew Jackson.

Insane with jealousy, Robards petitioned the Virginia assembly for a divorce. The petition was granted, but all it did was give the husband the right to go into court and get a divorce. It was falsely reported in the Cumberland settlements that Robards had been granted a divorce, but he made no move to take the case into court.

In August, 1791, Rachel Robards and Andrew Jackson were married in Natchez, Mississippi. Not until two years later, in the fall of 1793, did they learn that Rachel had never been legally divorced. A second wedding was proposed by Jackson's close friend, John Overton, but Jackson at first refused. Before God, he declared, and in "the understanding of every person in the country," Rachel had become his wife at Natchez. But in January, 1794, Jackson and Rachel were married a second time, and according to tradition the ceremony was performed by the Rev. Thomas B. Craighead.

Man never loved woman more than Andrew Jackson loved his wife, before and after death took her from him. And Rachel returned his love. The situation of the Hermitage, the beauty of its garden, the gracious atmosphere of the place are reflections of their love.

Authoritative historians say that Rachel and Andrew were blameless in all the events surrounding their courtship and marriage. But Jackson's political enemies never let him forget. With pen and pistols he defended Rachel's honor as long as he lived— but the shafts of his political foes robbed her of some of the happiness that she deserved, and perhaps shortened her life.

JACKSON'S DUELS

Andrew Jackson was a man of his times, and dueling, though frowned upon by thoughtful men and outlawed in Tennessee, was still an accepted way of settling differences between gentlemen. Some writers assert that Jackson was involved in "many" duels. The facts are that he fought one serious, formal duel (with Dickinson), acted as a second in one duel (Carroll and Benton), engaged in one public brawl, or gunfight (with the Bentons), and engaged in one harmless affair in which both participants fired into the air.

This last mentioned encounter was Jackson's first duel, and it occurred when he was a hot-blooded young man of 21, briefly practicing law in Jonesborough, Tennessee, while en route to the Cumberland country. Col. Waightstill Avery, a veteran lawyer, affronted the young attorney with what Jackson took to be an aspersion upon his knowledge of law. He retaliated by accusing Avery of taking illegal fees, and an exchange of insults soon brought the two men on the "field of honor." Through the good offices of friends both combatants were persuaded to fire into the air, and the affair ended with nothing worse than the popping of pistols.

Jackson engaged in a famous feud with Gov. John Sevier, who insulted Judge Jackson in the street with a sneering reference to his marriage. Jackson wanted recourse to pistols, but Sevier found ways of avoiding a formal encounter—though he got the worst of a bitter confrontation.

The affair with Charles Dickinson, resulting in Dickinson's death, was a controversial event in Jackson's career. The young man, a favorite of Nashville society, had twice made off-color remarks about Rachel Jackson. Dickinson said he was drunk, and Jackson let it pass. But when the two men became further involved over the results of a horse race, an insulting "card" was printed in the Nashville newspaper, and a duel was inevitable.

At a meeting on Red River, across the Kentucky line, Dickinson seriously wounded Jackson. Jackson remained erect, despite the blow of the one-ounce ball. At the first attempt his pistol failed to fire, and with cool deliberation he re-cocked and fired a shot that fatally wounded Dickinson.

Some biographers have thought that Jackson should have spared his adversary after the first mis-fire. But with Dickinson's bullet burning into his breast, Dickinson's slander burning in his brain, and a great anger for Dickinson burning in his heart, Jackson pulled the trigger again, and lived with the consequences. His wound was serious, and in some quarters, his reputation suffered.

The affair with the Bentons was the result of another duel, fought between Jackson's protege, William Carroll, and Jesse Benton. When Jackson tried to "cowhide" Thomas Hart Benton at Nashville's old City Hotel, a general fight ensued, in which Jackson was again seriously wounded, supposedly by Jesse Benton. Jackson and Thomas Benton, who had been friends before the encounter, became friends again in later years, and among Jackson's last words was a message of gratitude to Tom Benton.

Jackson's duels were over-emphasized, during and after his lifetime, because of his rise to fame. Even admiring biographers do not assert that he was blameless, but none dispute that he did what he thought to be right. That he lived to rise above the memory of these unfortunate encounters, and to regain whatever esteem he may have lost as a result of them, is but another tribute to the greatness of the man.

MILITARY CAREER

Although without formal education in military science and tactics, it was Andrew Jackson's achievements as a military commander that won him national recognition and put him on the road to the White House. His public career being somewhat in the doldrums at the time, it was the War of 1812 with Britain that finally gave him the opportunity to serve his country in the field. Not all his battles were clear-cut victories, but none were defeats, and he was to emerge as the most able field commander in the country.

Jackson had to make his own military opportunities, and often at his own expense. After leading a fruitless expedition to Natchez early in 1813, Jackson found himself ordered by the War Department to dismiss his troops and "deliver over to Major General James Wilkinson all articles of public property." He promptly marched his men back to Nashville, and it was on that bitter, hungry journey that Jackson's soldiers first called their commander a name that would be known to every American—Old Hickory.

In the fall of that year, with the uprising of the Creek Indians and the massacre at Fort Mims, Jackson began the campaign that would lead him, eventually, to New Orleans and military glory. It was a long, bitter, mutinous and at times ill-starred campaign. Famine, short enlistments and faint hearts were more dangerous than the Creeks, but it was during these dark days that Jackson showed the stuff he was made of.

He used every possible device to hold his army together. He moved swiftly and struck hard, keeping the Creeks off balance, and by the force of his will he inspired the governor of Tennessee to bestir himself, and send more troops.

Tallushatchee, Talladega, Emuckfaw Creek and Enotachopco were preludes to the showdown at Tohopeka, or the Horseshoe Bend. Here, on March 27, 1814, Jackson cornered 800 Creek warriors behind a barricade, with the Tallapoosa River at their backs. When the sun set almost all the Creeks were dead, on the field or in the river, and the power of the Red Sticks was broken.

The American government had at last found a general, who could win battles, and in the fall of 1814 Andrew Jackson, now a major general in the U. S. Army, arrived at Mobile with the Third U. S. Infantry to guard against an expected British assault on the Gulf Coast. Early in November he stormed and took Pensacola, a Spanish possession used by the British as a concentration point. The Spaniards surrendered, and the British retired to their ships. Late in the month Jackson moved toward New Orleans, where he expected considerable reinforcements from Tennessee, under William Carroll and John Coffee.

In New Orleans Jackson was lionized as the only man who could save the city from the expected British attack. He set about the defense of the the port with great energy, finding the topography of the country little understood, and offering a number of routes to an invading army. In mid-December the British entered Lake Borgne, and prepared to descend on the city.

Jackson worked feverishly to build up his army. Besides his Tennessee and Kentucky frontiersmen he had New Orleans militia, some Baratarian freebooters including Dominique You and Jean Lafitte, Mississippi Dragoons, some friendly Choctaws and the Seventh Regiment of regular U. S. infantry.

When he heard of the British landing from Lake Borgne Jackson determined on an immediate attack. His remarks have become a part of the American military tradition: "By the Eternal, they shall not sleep on our soil," and "I will smash them, so help me God!" The attack, delivered smartly on the evening of December 23, did not smash the British, but it stopped them in their tracks, checked the momentum of their advance on New Orleans, and set the stage for a major battle.

The main British attack came early on the morning of January 8, 1815. "Up until now," wrote Marquis James, "Andrew Jackson's life had been a preface to this moment."

Gen. Sir Edward Pakenham, the British commander, threw about six thousand men against Jackson's mud parapet, which extended a mile and a half from the Mississippi on the British left to a swamp on their right. A part of the British force was thrown west of the river in an attempt to enfilade Jackson's line, which sheltered about 5,000 men. The remainder of the Red Coat force moved against the two ends of the American breastworks.

Jackson's frontier riflemen and 25 pieces of artillery opened up with deadly effect, and Pakenham's attack was a miserable failure. The British ranks melted away under "the most rapid and destructive fusillade ever poured into a column of soldiers," and Pakenham was among the slain.

By half past eight in the morning the battle was over, and the British had suffered a crushing defeat. Total British casualties were 2,037. American losses totaled 71, of which 13 were killed.

The Encyclopedia Britannica says the battle had no effect on the outcome of the war, the peace treaty having been signed at Ghent 15 days earlier. The fact is that the treaty had not been ratified, and the British had always denied the validity of the Louisiana Purchase by the United States.

Had Pakenham defeated Jackson, taken New Orleans and blocked up the Mississippi, it requires little imagination to realize that the British Empire builders of that day would never have given up the port.

The aftermath of the battle was not all pleasant. Jackson's restrictive measures in the city got him into trouble with Federal Judge Dominick Hall, and the general was eventually fined $1,000 and costs for contempt of court. In later years the U. S. Congress repaid the fine, with interest.

The Battle of New Orleans set Jackson's star over the White House and restored the military pride of the nation—somewhat tarnished by the burning of the national capital by British raiders. The victory made the Mississippi an American river, and turned the eyes of Americans toward the Pacific.

The Florida campaign of 1818 ended General Jackson's military career. In the spring of that year, leading an army of 800 U. S. regulars and 900 Georgia militia, Jackson entered Spanish Florida to find Seminole warriors melting away before his advance, without offering battle.

The Spanish minister, however, was soon demanding "a prompt restitution of St. Mark's, Pensacola, Barrancas, and all other places wrested by General Jackson from the crown of Spain. I demand . . . punishment of the general."

In the course of the campaign Jackson captured Alexander Arbuthnot, a trader with the Indians, and Robert Armbrister, an English officer and soldier of fortune. The trader was charged with inciting the Indians to war, and Armbrister with "assuming command of the Indians in war with the United States."

Jackson convened a military court which sentenced Arbuthnot to be hanged. Armbrister was sentenced to be shot, and upon reconsideration, to 50 lashes and confinement for one year. Jackson approved Arbuthnot's sentence, and in Armbrister's case, the first of the two decisions. Both men were executed.

When Spain protested Jackson's invasion President James Monroe and Secretary of War John C. Calhoun explained that Jackson had acted beyond his authorization, and the captured cities were returned to Spain. It was only through the intervention of Secretary of State John Quincy Adams, who strongly defended Jackson's course, that the general escaped censure. But the fact was, as noted by historian Marquis James, that the administration "gave its consent" to Jackson's expedition into Florida, and then tried to wash its hands of the affair.

In January of 1819 Jackson went to Washington to defend his conduct against the charges of ambitious politicians William Crawford and Henry Clay. In a series of showdown votes, the U. S. House of Representatives approved Jackson's conduct of the Florida campaign.

In a moving farewell to his troops, Major General Andrew Jackson resigned from the army on June 1, 1821, soon after accepting the office of Governor of the Florida Territory. The old soldier laid down his sword with the stern admonition that what the army needed most was better discipline.

Statesman, farmer, lawyer, merchant—perhaps it was the military life that Jackson loved most. In the eyes of Tennesseans, and of most Americans, it was not the office of the presidency that made Jackson a great man, to be loved and remembered. It was rather Jackson's greatness that led him to the highest office in the land—a greatness won as a leader of men on the field of battle.

Eight

JACKSON AS PRESIDENT

At 21 Andrew Jackson had been an attorney general, at 31 a judge of the superior court and a United States Senator. He had served as a member of the convention which adopted the first constitution of Tennessee in 1796, and he was the first man to represent the state in the U. S. House of Representatives.

In the latter office Jackson was an active member. He offered a petition for the building of a road from Virginia and Maryland to the Northwest Territory. He urged that the federal government assume the expenses for an Indian campaign commanded by John Sevier and Hugh L. White, and he went on record as opposing a laudatory "farewell address" to George Washington.

In October of 1823 the Tennessee legislature, in session at Murfreesboro, elected Jackson U. S. Senator, and it was while serving in this office that he first became a candidate for President in 1824. In this election Jackson received the largest number of popular and electoral votes, but no candidate having a majority, the winner was decided by the House of Representatives, which chose John Quincy Adams on the first ballot.

Defeated candidate Henry Clay of Kentucky had thrown his influence to Adams to bring about Jackson's defeat, and Adams now made Clay secretary of state. Jackson denounced this combination as a deal between the "Puritan and the Blackleg," and for four long years his supporters repeated the charge of "monstrous union" and "corrupt bargain." In 1828, by an overwhelming vote, Adams was defeated and Jackson elevated to the presidency. Before he could ride to Washington for his inauguration, Mrs. Jackson died suddenly, and was buried in the Hermitage garden. With a heavy heart, the old hero took up the burdens of the nation's highest office.

Jackson became President with the following statement of principles:

"The Federal Constitution must be obeyed, state rights preserved, our national debt must be paid, direct taxes and loans avoided, and the Federal Union preserved. These are the objects I have in view, and regardless of all consequences will carry into effect."

These policies Jackson proceeded to carry out. He did pay off the national debt, and the national government accumulated a surplus of $35,000,000 during the last years of his administration. This surplus, by act of Congress, was distributed to the various states, giving Jackson a record of fiscal achievement unparalleled in the history of the United States.

The so-called Peggy Eaton affair occurred when wives of Jackson's first cabinet members refused social recognition to the wife of John H. Eaton of Tennessee, secretary of war. The cabinet was greatly strengthened by resignations and new appointments in 1831, making it one of the strongest in American history.

In 1832, under the leadership of John C. Calhoun, South Carolina attempted to nullify the U. S. tariff laws. Calhoun contended that sovereign states might nullify acts of Congress which were in violation of the Constitution.

Jackson now allied himself with Daniel Webster and the forces of Union as opposed to the nullification doctrine. At a dinner honoring Thomas Jefferson the President struck a heavy blow at the doctrine of nullification with his famous toast:

"Our Federal Union—it must be preserved."

It was during Jackson's first administration that the Democratic or Republican party divided into "Jacksonian Democrats" and "National Republicans" later called Whigs. The Whig party might properly be called the "Anti-Jackson" party, and one Jackson biographer, Senator Kenneth D. McKellar, referred to them simply as "the enemies of Jackson."

In Jackson's later years the Whigs, led by men jealous of his reputation, were particularly powerful in Tennessee. They fought him at every turn, carrying the state for Hugh L. White against Democrat Martin Van Buren in 1836. In 1840 the Whigs carried the state for William Henry Harrison. Four years later their bitterness reached its limit when they again carried the state for Henry Clay, Jackson's old enemy, while the country was sending Tennessee's own candidate, Democrat James K. Polk, to the White House. McKellar described Clay as a shop-worn candidate who had been on every side of every public question.

In 1832 Jackson ran for re-election on a platform of opposition to the Bank of the United States, and having defeated Henry Clay by a great majority, he proceeded to end the bank's existence with the withdrawal of government deposits. His long battle against the bank and final victory was considered one of the great achievements of Jackson's career as President.

For many years school textbooks accused President Jackson of introducing the "spoils system" of office holding into American politics. Modern historians, however, refute the charge. Out of 10,000 government office holders he dismissed less than 10 per cent.

As President, Andrew Jackson forced the removal of the Cherokee Indians to Western reservations. He favored the annexation of Texas to the Union and appointed a charge d'affaires to the Republic of Texas.

The Encyclopedia Britannica notes that "Jackson is perhaps the only President of whom it may be said that he went out of office far more popular than he was when he entered. He left his party strong, perfectly organized and enthusiastic . . . His name still remained a spell to conjure with."

In his farewell address President Jackson looked a quarter of a century down the years to a time when the Union might be broken apart, and he warned against the danger.

"In the union of these states," he said, "there is a sure foundation for the brightest hopes of freedom, and for the happiness of the people. At every hazard, and by every sacrifice, this Union must be preserved.

"If the Union is once severed, the line of separation will grow wider and wider, and the controversies which are now debated and settled in the halls of legislation, will then be tried in the fields of battle, and determined by the sword."

With a final warning against sectionalism, a stern defense of the right of states to regulate their own affairs and a plain statement on the limitation of the powers of federal government, Andrew Jackson ended his public career, and turned his face toward the Hermitage.

THE HERMITAGE

The Hermitage toward which Andrew Jackson turned his face in 1837 was almost a new house, completed two years before after the disastrous fire of 1834. This fire ruined much of the interior of the house, sparing only the dining room wing. The walls and foundations were used in the new building, as was much material from the old building.

When Andrew Jackson and Rachel were first married in 1791 they made their home with Rachel's mother, the widow of John Donelson, who lived north of the Cumberland River near the present highway from Nashville to Gallatin. On April 30, 1793, for the sum of one hundred pounds, Jackson bought the Poplar Grove tract in Jones' (now Hadley's) Bend, and it was here, late in 1793 or early in 1794 that Andrew and Rachel built the first home of their own. It was called Poplar Grove, later changed to Poplar Flat.

At this time there was still danger of Indians on outlying farms, and as late as September, 1794, there were reports to the War Department of Indian attacks in the vicinity. It was during this summer that a frontier army assembled at Mud Tavern, near the present town of Donelson, for the Nickajack expedition, a final campaign that made Middle Tennessee relatively safe from bandit Indians.

During the First World War the site of the Jacksons' Poplar Flat home was swallowed up by the "Old Hickory" powder plant. The only trace of the old home left today is a deep, stone-lined well, known to old residents of the community as "Jackson's Water Well."

On March 7, 1796, Andrew Jackson bought the Hunter's Hill tract of 640 acres from John Shannon for $700. This home, about two miles from the present Hermitage, was on land formerly owned by Mrs. Jackson's first husband, Lewis Robards. Hunter's Hill was considered a notable home for its day and time, offering an inspiring view of the river. Jackson established a general store at Hunter's Hill, and according to tradition both he and Rachel waited on the trade.

A financial panic swept the country in 1798-99 and young Andrew Jackson suffered serious losses. When a wealthy Philadelphia merchant failed, Jackson, who had accepted his notes, went heavily in debt. He struggled to pay every cent, and did. But in the process he was forced to sell Hunter's Hill. That same year, 1804, he bought from Nathaniel Hays for $3,400 the 420-acre tract which was to become the present Hermitage.

Jackson now moved his store to the famous Clover Bottom, on the banks of Stone's River near the Lebanon road. Here he had a variety of enterprises, in partnership with others, including a tavern, race track and boat yard.

In those days the Hermitage consisted of a group of log buildings built near each other. The largest was a two-story blockhouse,

MRS RACHEL JACKSON
PAINTED BY RALPH E. W. EARL

Rachel Jackson, daughter of Col. John Donelson, a founder of Nashville, married Andrew Jackson in 1791. The couple, devoted to each other for 37 years, were parted by Rachel's death in 1828.

GENERAL ANDREW JACKSON
PAINTED BY RALPH E. W. EARL

Andrew Jackson's achievements as a general of the U. S. Army won him great national recognition and contributed to his later being elected to the Presidency of the United States. Jackson's most famous military victory was the Battle of New Orleans in 1815.

GENERAL ANDREW JACKSON ON SAM PATCH
(See Back Cover)
PAINTED BY RALPH E. W. EARL

General Jackson, in full military uniform, is depicted astride Sam Patch, a beautiful horse presented to him in 1833 by the citizens of Pennsylvania.

Mrs. Rachel Jackson
Painted by Ralph E. W. Earl

Advice to Andrew Jackson by his Mother

In 1781, Andrew Jackson, then 14 years of age, enlisted in the American army; was captured and thrown into prison where he had smallpox. His mother, Elizabeth Hutchinson Jackson, through exchange arranged for his release and nursed him back to health. Responding to an urgent appeal, she left him to go to Charleston to nurse some sick neighbors who were confined there on a British hospital ship. This errand of mercy cost her life. She caught yellow fever and died.

Almost her last words to her young son were:

"Andrew, if I should not see you again, I wish you to remember and treasure up some things I have already said to you; in this world you will have to make your own way. To do that you must have friends. You can make friends by being honest and you can keep them by being steadfast. You must keep in mind that friends worth having will in the long run expect as much from you as they give to you. To forget an obligation or to be ungrateful for a kindness is a base crime—not merely a fault or a sin but an actual crime. Men guilty of it sooner or later must suffer the penalty. In personal conduct be always polite but never obsequious. None will respect you more than you respect yourself. Avoid quarrels as long as you can without yielding to imposition. But sustain your manhood always. Never bring a suit in law for assault and battery or for defamation. The law affords no remedy for such outrages that can satisfy the feelings of a true man. Never wound the feelings of others. Never brook wanton outrage upon your own feelings. If ever you have to vindicate your feelings or defend your honor, do it calmly. If angry at first, wait till your wrath cools before you proceed."

These words were repeated by General Jackson on his birthday March 15th, 1815, at New Orleans to three members of his military family. Major John H. Eaton, Major Wm. B. Lewis and Captain W. O. Butler. "Gentlemen", said General Jackson, "I wish she could have lived to see this day. There never was a woman like her. She was gentle as above and brave as a lioness. Her last words have been the law of my life."

General Andrew Jackson
A great national figure and military hero.
Painted by Ralph E. W. Earl

built to resist Indian attacks, where Rachel and Andrew lived. Guests were accommodated in three smaller log cabins. A part of this log cabin home still stands to the rear of the Hermitage.

In this log establishment the Jacksons received such distinguished guests as Aaron Burr and President James Monroe, and it was to this frontier home that Major General Jackson returned after his famous victory at New Orleans.

In 1818, when Andrew Jackson was nationally known, and prospering with a boom cotton market, Rachel Jackson selected the site where the present Hermitage stands. The original house, completed in 1819, was a square brick structure, probably designed by Jackson himself and built by skilled slave labor, perhaps under the direction of a master builder. In this comfortable but unpretentious home the Jacksons lived for nine happy years, until Rachel's death parted them in 1828. As President-elect Jackson sat at her bier he said: "What are all the world and its honors to me since she is taken from me?"

In 1831, while Jackson was President, the Hermitage was extensively remodeled and improved. The two wings and front and back porticos were added, the front portico only one story high. The wings were gabled at front and back, instead of the present flat roofs. A new kitchen and smokehouse were built. The dining room would seat 100 persons.

Andrew Jackson's adopted son, Andrew Jackson, Jr., had married Sarah York of Philadelphia that year, and brought his bride to the Hermitage. Sarah was a great favorite of the President, and probably he intended the Hermitage remodeling as a sort of a wedding present for her.

Sarah York Jackson became the mistress of the Hermitage, and except for brief absences she lived there, as wife and widow, until her death in 1888. This gracious, warm-hearted woman was eminently fitted to be mistress of the Hermitage. Andrew Jackson loved her as his own daughter, and perhaps she came as near as any woman could to filling the void in his heart left by the death of his own beloved Rachel. For a time she served as President Jackson's official hostess of the White House.

It was in October of 1834 that the roof of the Hermitage caught fire from a chimney. According to a newspaper report "the entire edifice, with the exception of a room attached to the northern end and used as a dining room was in a few hours destroyed." Much of the furniture on the lower floor was saved.

"Tell Sarah to cease to mourn its loss," wrote Andrew Jackson to his son, "I will have it rebuilt." This he did, at a cost of

$6,500, plus the cost of new furnishings. The rebuilding of his home, at this time of life, was a financial blow to Jackson, and it meant that he would come home in 1837 with little money in pocket, and heavy burdens to shoulder in the last years of his life.

The Hermitage was rebuilt by the carpenter-contractors Joseph Reiff and William C. Hume, who, about the same time, were building the beautiful brick home at Tulip Grove, across Lebanon Road from the Hermitage.

Today Tulip Grove, as beautiful as it was when Emily Donelson lived there, is operated as a museum house by The Ladies' Hermitage Association.

General Jackson, who operated the Hermitage Plantation as a cotton, corn and hog farm, was the only man who could ever make it pay. When the general died in 1845 and was buried in the garden beside his beloved wife, he left behind an estate which, after debts were paid, was worth $150,000—a considerable legacy in those days. Andrew Jackson, Jr., was a kindly, personable man, but not a good manager, and the property slipped away from him. The Hermitage, famed for its hospitality in General Jackson's day, gradually declined.

In 1856, the Hermitage farm being heavily mortgaged, Andrew Jackson, Jr., conveyed to the state of Tennessee the Hermitage and 500 acres—the "south part" of what had been a 1200 acre farm—for the sum of $48,000. At that time it was the intention of the state to present the mansion and farm to the federal government as the site for a national military academy.

Andrew Jackson, Jr., and his family left the Hermitage in 1858, but at the invitation of Gov. Isham G. Harris they returned in 1860 to become custodians of the property until further plans could be made.

During the Civil War the Hermitage was protected by a guard of federal troops sent out from Nashville by Gen. George H. Thomas. A federal soldier stationed in Nashville remarked that "the place must have been a fine one in its palmy days, but now through neglect it's pretty well run to weeds."

Andrew Jackson, Jr., died at the Hermitage in 1865, leaving his widow, Mrs. Sarah Jackson, and her widowed sister, Mrs. Marion Adams, the sole occupants of the Hermitage. His death was the result of an unfortunate hunting accident in which he was fatally wounded. The daughter, Rachel, a favorite of General Jackson, had married Dr. John M. Lawrence. All the young men, the sons of Andrew and Sarah Jackson, as well as those of Mrs. Adams, five in number, joined the Confederate army. Only one, Col. Andrew Jackson, III, returned.

The State legislature allowed Mrs. Sarah Jackson to remain tenant at will, during her life, at the Hermitage. She died in 1888, her sister, Mrs. Adams, having preceded her to the grave. Both are buried in the garden.

Col. Andrew Jackson, III, after serving gallantly as colonel of artillery in the Confederate army, returned, the only surviving soldier of the Hermitage family, a released prisoner from Fort Warren, Mass. He remained with his mother during her life and by her will inherited the household furniture, mementos and relics of the old hero. Colonel Jackson died in Knoxville, Tenn., December 17, 1906, and was buried in the Hermitage garden by the side of his brother, Capt. Samuel Jackson. Andrew Jackson, IV, son of Col. and Mrs. Jackson, died in Los Angeles, California, in 1953, and is buried in the Hermitage garden. His brother, Albert Marble Jackson, was reputedly lost at sea.

THE LADIES' HERMITAGE ASSOCIATION

MRS. ANDREW JACKSON, III (Amy Rich), conceived the idea of The Ladies' Hermitage Association. The organizers were Andrew Jackson, III, Mrs. Mary C. Dorris, Mr. and Mrs. William A. Donelson.

In her book, "Preservation of the Hermitage," Mrs. Dorris gives a very modest account of her own part in the founding of the Association. The fact is that she was, from the first, an energetic and tireless worker in the project to save the Hermitage—perhaps the leading spirit of this dedicated group.

Mrs. Dorris' book is still the best authority on the early days of the Association. It is from her that we have the story of Jackson's slave, Uncle Alfred, who lived to be a venerable guide at the Hermitage. She tells us of the lighting of the Cornwallis candle on Jackson Day, and informs us that the official colors of the Association are green and white, its badge a wreath of hickory leaves.

On February 19, 1889, Mrs. Rachel J. Lawrence, Mary W. May, Mrs. Mary Hadley Clare, Mrs. E. L. Nicholson, Miss Louise Grundy Lindsley, Mrs. Henry Heiss, and Mrs. Dorris applied to the State of Tennessee and were granted a charter incorporating The Ladies' Hermitage Association. The objects of the Association stated in the charter were to purchase from the State of Tennessee certain land, including the residence and tomb of Andrew Jackson, and to "beautify, preserve, and adorn the same throughout all coming years, in a manner most befitting the memory of that great man, and commensurate with the gratitude of his countrymen."

The General Assembly of the State of Tennessee, on April 5, 1889, conveyed to trustees for The Ladies' Hermitage Association twenty-five acres of the Hermitage farm, including the house, tomb, and surrounding buildings.

Dr. and Mrs. J. Berrien Lindsley rendered very efficient service in securing from the State legislature the original conveyance of twenty-five acres to The Ladies' Hermitage Association.

The General Assembly of the State of Tennessee (Chapter No. 27, Public Acts of Tennessee, 1923), at the earnest solicitation of the officers and directors of The Ladies' Hermitage Association, conveyed 232-5/10 acres of The Hermitage farm, located in the Fourth Civil District of Davidson County, Tennessee, to the Board of Trustees for The Ladies' Hermitage Association, to the end that "said The Ladies' Hermitage Association be permitted and encouraged to preserve and beautify same, so as to display the respect, love, and affection which a grateful State and people cherish for their illustrious hero and statesman, Andrew Jackson."

The General Assembly of the State of Tennessee in 1935, by Public Act, conveyed the remainder of the original 500-acre Hermitage farm to the Board of Trustees to be maintained under the care and custody of The Ladies' Hermitage Association. The Hermitage farm is now under the supervision of The Ladies' Hermitage Association for preservation as a perpetual memorial. In 1960 the Association acquired 125 acres adjoining the north boundry as protection against future industrial or housing developments, bringing the total acreage to 625.

The furniture and relics were in the Hermitage at the time of the organization of The Ladies' Hermitage Association in 1889, and Col. Andrew Jackson gave the Association an option upon them. But failing to raise the necessary money after four years' trial, the entire collection of relics and furniture was removed in 1893 by the owner, Col. Andrew Jackson, to Cincinnati, where he had them on exhibition for pay. This venture was not a success, so they were returned to Nashville. From this collection and from various members of the family and others, the Association has bought the relics which it now owns, and which so beautifully adorn the residence where they first were placed.

The Association in its early years put forth untiring efforts to raise the funds necessary to restore the mansion and collect the original furnishings and relics. It inaugurated various enterprises, such as lectures, concerts, balls, etc.

On October 22, 1907, President Theodore Roosevelt visited the Hermitage, and in a speech on that occasion promised government. aid. He incorporated the matter in his annual message, and through the efforts of Senator James B. Frazier and Rep. John W. Gaines, both of whom were trustees, Congress made an appropriation of $5,000 to repair and improve the Hermitage. The present sources of revenue are admission fees, souvenir shop sales, and Association membership dues.

The collection of relics and furniture now in the house is the result of years of effort of The Ladies' Hermitage Association. It is interesting to note, in this connection, that the Hermitage is the only great national shrine in this country having original furnishings throughout. All furnishings in the house belonged to General Jackson, with the exception of a few articles which, in each case, are noted in the catalogue.

In 1961, the National Park Service of the U. S. Department of the Interior designated the Hermitage as a Registered National Historic Landmark.

For forty-five years following the opening of the Hermitage to the public, Mr. and Mrs. T. L. Baker served as careful and dedicated custodians of the buildings and grounds. They were succeeded by their son, Andrew Jackson Baker, who was born in the Hermitage, and his wife, and it is due to their dedication and interest that the Hermitage has maintained its reputation as the nation's best-kept shrine. Due to ill health, Mr. Baker resigned in 1963. Stephen S. Lawrence served as Director until 1967. The present director is James E. Arnold.

THE GROUNDS

Today the Hermitage farm, containing 625 acres, is operated as a grass and beef cattle farm. The operation is quite different, and done with far less labor, than in Jackson's day of cotton and corn farming. Game chickens and horses are usually to be seen on the farm—reminiscent of the Hermitage when the General was master of the plantation.

Some of the stately trees that beautify the Hermitage were there in Jackson's time, and some planted since have historical significance. The tall cedars that line the guitar-shaped driveway were planted in the summer of 1837 by Ralph E. W. Earl, Jackson's friend and "artist in residence" at the Hermitage. Earl suffered a heat stroke while planting these trees, and died of an illness which followed. He is buried in the garden.

To the east of the tomb, in the garden, is a short, thick-set row of hickory trees. These trees grew from a parcel of hickory nuts sent Jackson in 1830 by an admirer in Ulster, New York. Jackson wrote that he would have them planted to "encircle the tomb" of his departed wife.

On the western edge of the front lawn are straight rows of hardwood trees from the battlefields that made Jackson famous. Chalmette, the Horseshoe, Fort Jackson and Talladega are represented in the group, and the old driveway they once bordered has been called "Jackson's War Road."

TULIP GROVE

Now operated as a museum house by The Ladies Hermitage Association, Tulip Grove stands on an elevated, wooded lawn across Lebanon Road from the Hermitage. The house today is just as it was when its first owners, Andrew Jackson Donelson and his wife, Emily, lived there in 1836.

The story of Tulip Grove is the story of the beautiful, red-haired Emily, who served her beloved "Uncle Jackson" as hostess of the White House, feuded with him over Peggy Eaton and returned to Tennessee.

A reconciliation followed, and Emily was once again hostess at the White House. It was then that Andrew Jackson contributed to the construction of Tulip Grove which the Donelsons erected using the same master builders, Reiff and Hume, who later rebuilt the Hermitage after the fire in 1834.

The final chapter of Emily's life was a tragic one. While her husband labored in Washington she waited, desperately ill, for his return to Tulip Grove. Finally, at Christmas time in 1836, he reached home—too late to take her in his arms again. Dead of tuberculosis at 29, she had lived in her new house for only six months. Her grief-stricken husband arrived only in time for her funeral.

First called Poplar Grove for its beautiful tulip poplar trees, the name Tulip Grove was suggested by President Martin Van Buren while visiting in the home in 1842.

Andrew Jackson Donelson's second marriage in 1841 was to Mrs. Elizabeth Martin Randolph, who was the mistress of Tulip Grove until 1858. Numerous descendants of this union survive today.

Donelson represented President Tyler as charge d'affaires to the Republic of Texas in 1844 and was instrumental in negotiating the annexation of Texas. In 1846, President James K. Polk appointed him as Minister to Prussia.

In 1856, Donelson was an unsuccessful candidate for vice president, running on the ticket with Millard Fillmore.

Tulip Grove is a Southern plantation house with tall Doric columns, showing the influence of early Greek Revival. A spiral staircase ascends to the third floor. The front hall was hand painted by Ralph E. W. Earl to resemble blocks of Italian marble.

Tulip Grove was acquired in March, 1964, by The Ladies' Hermitage Association from Mrs. Jane Berry Buntin. The work of restoration is being continued, and furnishings of the house include several original and antique pieces. The portrait of Emily Donelson which hangs in the hall is a copy of one done by Earl.

A Guide To The Hermitage

THE GROUNDS

THE CARRIAGE HOUSE

In 1897, Col. Andrew Jackson, from whom most of the relics were purchased, sold to the Association the interesting old coach used by Jackson at the White House for state, ceremonial, and social purposes and for several trips to the Hermitage. The trip to the Hermitage took thirty days' time. His journeys were a continual ovation.

The skeleton of the phaeton is all that is left of the beautiful light carriage presented to General Jackson by the "Democratic-Republican" citizens of New York City. It was made from timbers taken from the old ship Constitution. The phaeton in which General Jackson rode with Martin Van Buren to the latter's inauguration was damaged by fire in Cincinnati, where the Jackson relics were stored before being acquired by The Ladies' Hermitage Association. A dim painting of the ship is still visible on the side panel of the phaeton.

(Photograph is on wall.)

Stone doorstep in front of carriage house was presented to Col. W. W. Parks by General Jackson. Given to The Ladies' Hermitage Association by his granddaughters, Misses Annie and Grace Handly.

Display boards on the walls show photostats of the Library of Congress letters of Rachel Jackson, personal accounts of life at the Hermitage taken from letters and histories, and pamphlets relating to the life and times of President Andrew Jackson, presented to the Hermitage by C. Lawrence Winn, great-grandson of Andrew Jackson, Jr.

Anvil, used in shoeing General Jackson's race horses.

Carpenter's plane, said to have been used by William McCreary in building the Hermitage. Given by Stanley F. Horn.

THE SMOKEHOUSE

Immediately behind the kitchen is the original brick smokehouse—empty now, but in the General's time filled with the great supply of hams and bacon needed for the feeding of a large household and a great number of slaves—not to mention the numerous guests. Today only its dark, smoke stained rafters remain to tell of all the succulent country hams that once hung there.

THE GARDEN AND THE TOMB

To the east of the mansion is the flower garden which General Jackson had laid out in 1819 for his wife, Rachel, whose chief interest it was.

It was designed by William Frost, a well-known English land-scapist, and it is considered by authorities to be an outstanding example of early American garden design.

More than an acre in area, the garden contains about fifty varieties of old-fashioned plants and great hickory and magnolia trees planted by General Jackson.

Guests at The Hermitage wrote of the flowers Mrs. Jackson gathered here and brought to them. Later, General Jackson referred to the garden as her monument and said. "Her memory will remain fresh there as long as life lasts."

Drawing of the Garden

Other interesting varieties of trees in the garden and on the grounds have markers showing their common and botanical names.

Copy of an old English sundial given by Thomas H. Berry. Base given by James W. Pearre.

The tomb of General and Mrs. Jackson is in the southeast corner of the garden, and many other members of their family and household are buried in the plot nearby.

The tomb was built by General Jackson in 1831 and was erected over his wife, with a vault for himself.

The inscription on General Jackson's tomb is:

GENERAL ANDREW JACKSON
Born March 15, 1767
Died June 8, 1845

The inscription on Mrs. Jackson's tomb was written by her husband, and is as follows:

"Here lie the remains of Mrs. Rachel Jackson, wife of President Jackson, who died the 22nd of December, 1828. Age, 61 years. Her face was fair, her person pleasing, her temper amiable, her heart kind; she delighted in relieving the wants of her fellow creatures, and cultivated that divine pleasure by the most liberal and unpretending methods; to the poor she was a benefactor; to the rich an example; to the wretched a comforter; to the prosperous an ornament; her piety went hand in hand with her benevolence, and she thanked her Creator for being permitted to do good. A being so gentle and so virtuous slander might wound, but could not dishonor. Even death, when he tore her from the arms of her husband, could but transport her to the bosom of her God."

The other graves on the plot are those of the adopted son, Andrew Jackson, Jr., and his wife, Mrs. Sarah York Jackson. Two infants lie buried there; also one son, Samuel Jackson, who was killed at Chickamauga; the grave of Dr. John M. Lawrence, who married Rachel, the idol of the old General's life. In February, 1923, the spirit of Mrs. Rachel Jackson Lawrence passed into the great beyond, and her body rests beside her husband and near her grandfather, the great hero, who affectionately looked upon and called her his "beloved little Rachel." The grave of Col. R. E. W. Earl, friend and companion of Jackson, is there. Farther apart from the other graves is that of Mrs. Marion Adams, the widowed sister of Mrs. Sarah Jackson who always resided with her, and whose family was reared at the Hermitage. On December 19, 1906, Col. Andrew Jackson, grandson, was laid beside his kindred dust in the garden, and his wife, Mrs. Amy Jackson, who died January 9, 1921, lies beside him. There are also the graves of John Marshall Lawrence, 1859-1926, and Thomas Donelson Lawrence, 1869-1942, sons of Mrs. Rachel Jackson Lawrence; and Anne Laurie Lawrence Smith, born at the Hermitage April 3, 1855, died February 4, 1937, and Sazie Lawrence Winn, born at the Hermitage March 15, 1854, died May 6, 1882, daughters of Mrs. Lawrence. Andrew Jackson, IV, son of Col. Andrew and Mrs. Amy Jackson, was buried here in 1953.

The grave of Uncle Alfred, freed slave who preferred to remain at the Hermitage and who wanted to be buried near General Jackson, is located to the north of the tomb in the garden.

The stone seat near the tomb is one of three presented to the Hermitage by Mrs. Marvin E. Holderness, Mr. Robert F. Jackson, Jr., and Mr. N. Baxter Jackson of New York, in memory of their mother, Mrs. Robert F. Jackson, who served as Regent of The Ladies' Hermitage Association. Mrs. Robert F. Jackson's grandmother, Mrs. Mary L. Baxter, served as first Regent 1889-1899.

OLD CARRIAGE HOUSE FROM HUNTER'S HILL

Log building used as a carriage house during Jackson's residence at Hunter's Hill, was moved from there and now located near the spring, used as a tool house.

The large barn was also moved to the Hermitage farm. It is used primarily for storage of hay, farm tools and stable. Here the farm staff tend a fine breed of game cocks. The stable, log barn and game cocks are reminiscent of the days when the Hermitage farm was the finest plantation in this area.

UNCLE ALFRED'S CABIN

Uncle Alfred was a favorite house-servant of General Jackson and often acted as his body-servant; he lived in a cabin in the rear yard. Born in 1803, he lived until 1901, and for many years entertained visitors when acting as guide through the Hermitage. At his request, he is buried near the Jackson tomb in the garden. This cabin has been furnished according to Uncle Alfred's time. In one of the rooms of the cabin is an old spinning jenny (original) presented by Mrs. W. B. Walton, a great-niece of Mrs. Jackson. This was inherited by Mrs. Walton from the family.

STONE SPRING HOUSE

One of Jackson's first acts, after building the first house to live in when he moved from Hunter's Hill, was to enclose the spring in a stone springhouse which Mrs. Jackson could use for keeping her milk and butter cold. Mrs. Jackson, who took an interest in the farm affairs, was especially proud of the spring which was and is an exceptionally good one.

THE LOG CABIN BY THE SPRING

This cabin was built in 1940 for use by The Ladies Hermitage Association. It consists of two spacious rooms and a kitchen equipped for simple cooking. It is used for the annual spring and fall outing of the Association, and members have the privilege of using the kitchen and one or both rooms for entertaining, upon application to the director and payment of a small fee. One of the rooms was furnished in memory of Mrs. Walter Stokes, former Regent, by her daughter, Mrs. W. H. Wemyss, and her son, Walter Stokes, Jr.

Twenty Five

The log cabin located at the northeast corner of the Hermitage grounds is part of the group of log houses which comprised the original Hermitage, where General and Mrs. Jackson resided from 1804 until 1819.

THE EARLY HERMITAGE

On March 7, 1796, Andrew Jackson bought the Hunter's Hill tract of 640 acres from John Shannon for the sum of $700. The Hunter's Hill house was located about two miles from the present Hermitage mansion.

A little more than a month and a half after the sale of the Hunter's Hill property, Andrew Jackson purchased the Hermitage estate. On the twenty-third of August, 1804, he paid Nathaniel Hays $3,400 for the 425-acre tract, "with its appurtenances," which was to become "The Hermitage." This reference to appurtenances supports the statement made in later years by Mrs. James K. Polk, wife of the eleventh President of the United States, that the Hermitage of the log cabin period "was not the commodious country house so familiar to devout Democrats in pilgrimages of later years. It was a group of log houses in close proximity to each other. The principal one had been built for a block-house in the days of Indian alarms, afterwards used as a store and, about 1804, converted into a dwelling. It, like all block-houses, was two stories high. Near it were three smaller houses, one story high, with low attics. These were used as lodgings for members of the family or guests."

Aaron Burr was entertained in these log buildings when he made his famous visits to the Hermitage in 1805 and 1806, and it was to this humble home that General Jackson returned after the Battle of New Orleans (January 8, 1815), which had made him the conquering hero and idol of the nation.

THE HERMITAGE CHURCH

Erected in 1823, across the Lebanon Road from The Hermitage Lane, this church was open to the public and services were held there until the recent fire. General Jackson, to please his devoutly religious wife, was the largest contributor to the building fund and always referred to it as "Mrs. Jackson's Church." In his latter years he was a faithful member, frequently arriving before the service with his man servant to see that the fires were properly made. Two log fireplaces were used for heat, home-made brick for flooring, and candles for light.

THE MUSEUM

The brick house now used as a museum was restored and built on the foundation of an original structure.

The Museum

South Room

1. Lace veil intended for Mrs. Rachel Jackson to wear at Jackson's inauguration in 1829, but her death occurred shortly before. The veil was presented by the ladies of Cincinnati. Each letter in the name Jackson is made from a different pattern of lace. The twenty-four stars above the name represent the 24 states, and in the center is an emblem of peace. This veil was inherited by Miss Mary Wilcox from her grandmother, Mrs. Andrew J. Donelson. Miss Wilcox presented the veil to the Tennessee Woman's Historical Association, which, in turn, presented it to the Hermitage Association.
2. Pictures of Jackson's cabinet members in 1829.
3. Part of original parlor draperies.
4. Part of original bedroom draperies.
5. Part of original curtains used in General Jackson's bedroom.
6. Portrait of Andrew Jackson by Ralph E. W. Earl.

Case No. 1

SHELF No. 1:

1. Gold sword presented to Andrew Jackson by the City of Philadelphia after the Battle of New Orleans.
2. Unique gun cane.
3. Turkish sword presented to General Jackson.
4. Cannon ball used in the Battle of New Orleans, January 8, 1815. Presented by Mrs. Burrell Jackson.
5. Sword captured at the Battle of New Orleans by General Jackson. Bought by the Association in 1897.
6. Cavalry sabre, captured at the Battle of New Orleans, bearing the coat of arms of the English Government and the initials G. R. (George Rex, III). Presented by W. E. Metzger.
7. Blade of sword presented to General Jackson by the citizens of New Orleans. This sword was bequeathed to Col. Andrew Jackson Coffee. Presented by Alexander D. Coffee.
8. Air gun and pump.

SHELF No. 2:

9. Leather shot pouch belonging to Andrew Jackson, Jr.
10. Sword said to have been used by Jackson at the Battle of New Orleans. Presented by Mrs. W. M. Calhoun.
11. Sword used by General Coffee at the Battle of New Orleans.
12. Piece of dining room floor laid in 1835 and removed in 1894.

Twenty Eight

13. Piece of the old bridge built by General Jackson's troops to cross a swamp at the head of the Bayou Grand near Fort Barrancas, Fla.

14. Gold sword presented to General Jackson July 4, 1822, by the State of Tennessee for his services at the Battle of New Orleans. It was bequeathed to Andrew J. Donelson, his former secretary. Purchased by The Ladies' Hermitage Association in 1940.

SHELF No. 3:

15. Wax candle found in Cornwallis' tent in Yorktown the night of his surrender to Washington. Presented to General Jackson who highly prized it and lighted it on each anniversary of the Battle of New Orleans.

16. Foresight of one of the cannons used at the Battle of New Orleans. Presented by Capt. E. W. Averell to Mrs. Bettie M. Donelson for the Hermitage Association.

17. Gold English dirk presented to Andrew Jackson at the Battle of New Orleans. Made by the English swordsmith Wooley, Deakin & Dutton.

18. Old door knob, removed from one of the doors.

19. Pieces of marble from the tomb of Mary Washington, mother of General George Washington; the cornerstone was laid by Jackson in 1833. Presented by Walter B. Parmer.

20. Military Regalia of General Jackson, presented by Joseph Horton Fall and John Hill Eakin.

21. United States cutlass used on the American Brig Carolina in a fight against the British in 1814-15, under General Jackson.

22. Silver mounted cane of General Jackson.

23. Italian carved cane, presented to General Jackson.

24. Gold-headed cane presented to General Jackson by Lt. Col. William L. Harneys, 2nd U. S. Dragoons, Sept. 30, 1838.

25. Walking cane of hickory.

26. Gun cane.

27. Cane made from wood that grew at the tomb of General Washington at Mt. Vernon. Presented by John Bigelow to General Jackson.

28. Folding bamboo camp chair.

29. Walking stick, presented to President Jackson by Thomas Hart Benton and John C. Calhoun and presented to the Hermitage Association by Mrs. J. A. Mitchell, Macon, Ga.

SHELF No. 4:

30. Shakespeare volume given and inscribed by Jackson to Henry L. Rucker of Cincinnati, 1837. Presented by Mrs. C. P. J. Mooney, 1950.

31. A British Dragoon flintlock holster pistol found on Jackson's battlefield at New Orleans in 1850. Presented by W. E. Metzger.

32. A stone from the grave of Andrew Jackson, father of General Jackson, who died in 1767. The grave is at Waxhaws Churchyard, S. C., and the stone was procured by Walter Lacoste Wilson and sent to Mrs. Rachel Jackson Lawrence, who presented it to the Hermitage Association.

33. Dueling pistol (one of a pair) owned by General Jackson. Presented by Miss Spon. The whereabouts of the other is not known.

34. A Jackson family pistol. Presented by Bettie Hoffstetter Reise.

35. English bayonet embedded in cypress root, found on the battlefield at New Orleans and presented to General Jackson in 1844.

36. The sword and belt of Capt. Samuel Jackson, C. S. A., grandson of General Jackson.

37. Powder flask used by General Jackson at the Battle of New Orleans.

38. Old pair of shears.

39. Rifle ornamented with plates of German silver, was given by General Jackson to Andrew Jackson, Jr. It was given by the Jacksons at the Hermitage in 1861 when a call was made for guns by the Southern Confederacy. Purchased at Clarksville, Tennessee, by a Federal officer whose son sold it to Mrs. B. F. Wilson. Presented by Mrs. Wilson to The Ladies' Hermitage Association.

Shelf No. 5:

40. Picture of Judge Spruce Macay, Justice of the North Carolina Supreme Court, law preceptor of Andrew Jackson. Gift of Archibald Henderson of North Carolina.

41. Jackson's license to practice law, 1787, North Carolina.

42. Commission of Major-General issued to Andrew Jackson, 1801, by Archibald Roane, Governor of Tennessee. Given by J. McGavock Dickinson.

43. Healy's account of his visit to the Hermitage to paint Jackson's portrait as commissioned by Louis Philippe.

44. Framed Declaration of Independence.

45. Letter to General Jackson from Bishop Henry Conwell, Roman Catholic Bishop of Philadelphia, written when he was in Rome, contained a picture of Pope Leo XII. Presented by Mrs. Bettie M. Donelson.

Case No. 2

Shelf No. 1:

1. Foot scraper, one of a pair used on the front porch.
1A. Original bedspread used until recently in Jackson's room, with initials R. J. in center.
2. Mexican leggings, hand-tooled leather. Presented to Major-General Andrew Jackson by Gov. Sam Houston.
3. Old account books of Jackson's & Hutchings' Store, December 26, 1803-June 15, 1804.
4. Part of one of the original lace curtains.
5. Fringe made and used by Rachel Jackson for a bedspread. Presented by Miss Emma Hoffstetter.
6. Sample of original chintz in Jackson's bedroom. Presented by Miss Cora Watson, having been given by Rachel Jackson to a member of her family, who were the Jacksons' neighbors.
7. Lace collar given by Rachel Jackson to Mrs. Governor Carroll, who gave it to her niece, Miss Bradford. At her death, at the age of 95, it was inherited by her niece, Mrs. Lizzie Miller Jones, who presented it to the Association.

Shelf No. 2:

8. Flat silver used at the Hermitage and at the White House, and two mahogany cases in which it was kept. Silver knife and corkscrew which belonged to Jackson. Presented by Mrs. Ramsey McIver, II.

Shelf No. 3:

9. Gold watch of the adopted son, Andrew Jackson, Jr.
9A. Memorandum book of Sarah York and Andrew Jackson, Jr., 1859, and his vest.
10. Daguerroetype of Captain Samuel Jackson, C.S.A., grandson of General Andrew Jackson, who was killed at the Battle of Chickamauga.
11. Two daguerreotypes of Andrew Jackson, Jr., adopted son of General and Mrs. Jackson.
12. Miniature of Mrs. Rachel Jackson Lawrence, only daughter of the Jacksons' adopted son. Her visiting card and that of her husband, which were given by Mrs. Richard Plater.
13. Portion of a gold link chain purchased by General Jackson in Philadelphia, 1831, and presented to his daughter-in-law, Sarah York Jackson. Given by Mrs. Joseph H. Thompson. The other portion of this chain was purchased from Miss Fannie O. Walton, great-great-niece of Mrs. Jackson.

14. The christening robe was worn by the children of Andrew and Sarah York Jackson.

15. The baby cap, which belonged to Rachel Jackson Lawrence, was given by her grandson, C. Lawrence Winn.

15A. Heart pin cushion, made by Rachel Jackson Lawrence of dress scraps from the Hermitage household. Given by Mrs. R. H. Oliphant, whose mother received it from a member of the Jackson family. The second heart pincushion, also made by Rachel Jackson Lawrence, the pearls from the Sarah York Jackson necklace, and the sample of the lining of the Jackson coach were acquired from Miss Effie McIver, whose forebears were close friends of the Jacksons.

16. Pearls which were given to Mrs. Sarah York Jackson, wife of Andrew Jackson, Jr., by President Jackson, when she went to the White House as a bride in 1831. She wore them to receptions given in her honor as a bride and also later as lady of the White House. The pearls have adorned seven brides in the immediate Jackson family. Purchased from the family by the Hermitage Association.

17. Small knife and fork set; given by General Jackson to his grandson, Andrew Jackson, III.

18. Invitation to General Jackson's funeral. Presented by Mrs. M. G. Buckner.

19. Presidential ticket (printed on satin) announcing Andrew Jackson's candidacy for the Presidency. Presented by N. B. Patterson, of Chicago. Printed by his grandfather, Col. J. B. Patterson, who was subsequently editor of the *Jacksonian*.

20. Bank book of General Jackson, dated 1810.

21. Physician's statement, 1826. Presented by Mrs. Leonard K. Whitworth.

22. Knife of General Jackson. Presented by J. H. Baker.

23. Engraving of Judge John Overton, Jackson's law partner and life-long friend. Presented by his great-grandson, J. McGavock Dickinson, Jr.

24. Letter from Andrew Jackson to the Hon. John Overton, August 21, 1831. Presented by Judge John H. DeWitt.

25. General Jackson's ruler, with outstanding dates of his life engraved thereon.

26. Pair of scales for weighing gold coin.

27. General Jackson's lancet, used by Dr. Esselman when he bled his patient. Presented by Mrs. Rachel Jackson Lawrence.

28. Original photograph of Dr. Benjamin Rohrer, physician to President Jackson during the entire time he was in the White House. Presented by Cordelia Jackson, 1922.

29. Latin Bible belonging to General Jackson, printed in Anno MDXCIII

30. Prayer book of General Jackson.

31. Bible of Rachel Jackson.

32. Brass compass of General Jackson which was like one used by George Washington at Valley Forge.

33. Hair of General Jackson in two frames, and lock of his hair presented by Mrs. Jack M. Bass.

34. Jackson's peace medal. Struck by the United States government and presented to all known chiefs of Indian tribes in the territories.

35. Jackson's temperance medal.

36. Billfold purchased by General Jackson in Tuscumbia, Ala., May 3, 1828.

37. Pocket comb belonging to General Jackson.

38. Miniature gloves made by an admirer and presented to Andrew Jackson.

39. Congressional medal, presented to Major-General Andrew Jackson after the Battle of New Orleans.

40. Picture of General Jackson and lock of his hair.

41. Porcelain French pipe.

42. Real amber pipe.

43. Pipe from the Alamo, San Antonio, Texas, where Davy Crockett died.

44. Turkish wooden pipe.

45. Two snuff boxes.

46. Sunglass used to light his pipe. Presented by Roy Roe of Mobile, Ala., to Mrs. George Nelson of Murfreesboro, who presented it to the Association.

47. Dutch pipe.

48. Jackson's watch, engraved: "Presented to General Andrew Jackson by W. W. C. January 12, 1815." Given by Rogers C. Caldwell in memory of his mother.

49. General Jackson's prayer book.

50. The stick pin worn by President Jackson. Presented by Mr. and Mrs. T. Graham Hall, in memory of his mother, Mrs. Jennie McIver Hall.

51. Gold-rimmed glasses worn by General Jackson until a few years before his death and presented by him to his daughter-in-law, Mrs. Sarah York Jackson. She gave them to the only granddaughter, Rachel Jackson, who presented them to John Marshall Lawrence. Purchased from him by the Association.

52. Miniature of Rachel Jackson, worn by General Jackson continuously until his death and only removed at night and placed with his Bible on a table by his bed.

SHELF No. 4:

53. "The Works of Lord Byron," presented to Jackson by Earl. Interesting letter from Byron to publishers of this volume is shown in Case H in opposite room.

54. Tortoise shell card case which belonged to R. E. W. Earl, given by Mrs. Stanley Horn.

54A. Card case and purse of Earl's, presented by C. L. Winn. Pen portrait of Earl.

55. Jackson Electoral Ticket, 1832. He was overwhelmingly re-elected, receiving 219 votes out of 286.

55A. Miniature of Jackson, given by Mrs. Benjamin A. Brakenbury, of Santa Barbara, Calif.

56. Jackson's Cabinet, 1829. Gift from Jackson to Major A. J. Donelson, Secretary to President Jackson.

57. New York, Nashville, Clarksville weekly papers of 1845, containing notices of the death of Jackson. Presented by W. M. Drane of Clarksville in 1920.

58. Badge worn at Jackson's funeral. Presented by Mrs. Frank Jefferson Blodgett of New York City, through Mrs. Lindsay Coleman of Nashville.

59. Badge used in commemoration of the death of Jackson. Presented by Charles Costleigh in memory of members of his family.

60. Letter from Thomas Jefferson, Monticello, 1821, regarding James Leander Cathcart.

61. Silver spoons, one of which is from a set of Jackson's spoons and the other from a set of Felix Grundy's. The handles were molded into Columbia Liberty Bells.

62. Silver cheese scoop, engraved, "G.W.C., Hermitage, Jan. 11, 1860," Editor of Harper's Weekly, to whom it was presented by the Jackson family.

62A. Hand fluting irons for curtains and bedding. Used by the Jackson family and presented by Mr. and Mrs. Jesse Stewart of Nashville.

63. Shaving case used by General Jackson.

64. Water color of Stockley place in Virginia, the home of Rachel Jackson's grandfather.

65. Gavel made of wood taken from the birthplace of Rachel Donelson, wife of Andrew Jackson. Presented by Mrs. Myrtle Blair Motley, Wm. Pitt Chapter, Chatham, Va.

66. Mortar and pestle used for compounding medicine.

67. Madonna and child breast pin belonged to Mrs. Sara York Jackson.

68. Rachel Jackson's night cap. Presented by Mrs. John H. Cunningham of San Antonio, great-granddaughter of Mrs. William Watson, a neighbor and friend of Mrs. Jackson who was with her during her last days and to whom Mrs. Jackson gave the cap.

68A. Preliminary sketch made by Sully of one of his portraits of Jackson.

69. Sewing case made and used by Rachel Jackson.

70. Long beaded purse, made by Rachel Jackson.

71. Spinning wheel in bottle presented to General Jackson.

72. Flat iron used at the Hermitage during Jackson's lifetime, presented by Andrew Jackson Baker, Jr.

73. Miniature of Jackson in youth.

74. Pair of gold-rimmed spectacles used by Mrs. Jackson.

75. Needlepoint bag.

76. Jackson beaded bag. Loaned by Tennessee State Library.

77. Miniature frame of onyx and gold inlay, containing lock of General Jackson's hair. Presented by Mrs. Joseph H. Crenshaw of Ft. Royal, Va.

78. Work bag of Rachel Jackson.

78A. Pearl comb, which belonged to Rachel Jackson. Given to her niece, Rachel Donelson Eckford, then to Mrs. H. J. Darden, who willed it to her cousin, Dr. M. M. Cullom. Presented by Dr. Cullom to the Association.

79. Rachel Jackson's pearl ring.

80. Set of mosaic jewelry consisting of belt clasp, necklace and ear rings, each medallion representing a different ancient temple, purchased by Andrew Jackson from widow of Stephen Decatur.

SHELF No. 5:

81. Part of letter written by Jackson to his wife, Rachel, regarding the Hermitage church and its pastor, the Rev. William Hume. Given by one of the latter's descendants, Leland Hume.

82. Painting of the Hermitage church, by Cornelius Hankins.

83. Poem on the death of Mrs. Jackson.

84. Letter from John Adams, Quincy, Mass., March 25, 1822 to James L. Cathcart.

85. Letter written by General Jackson to William Donelson, November 29, 1842. Presented by Miss Matilda Allison Porter, 1946.

86. Small portrait of Andrew Jackson, painted by Franklin Witcher of New York, for Jackson's Presidential campaign. Bought from a relative of the artist.

87. Springfield, Jefferson County, Miss., where Andrew and Rachel Jackson were married in 1791. Presented by Daniel Clay Bramlett of Woodville, Miss.

88. A letter of General Jackson to Mrs. Jackson, January 29, 1824. Presented by Judge John H. DeWitt.

89. Hermitage (or Ephesus) church membership roll 1824-1839 including the Jacksons, given by C. L. Winn.

90. A photostat of Jackson's list of contributions for repairs of the Hermitage church and suggested alterations made by Andrew Jackson Donelson, given by Stanley F. Horn.

Case No. 3

SHELF No. 1:

1. The green and white covered dishes, the six flowered soup plates, and the small knife and fork, which all belonged to the Jacksons, were given by Mr. and Mrs. T. Graham Hall, in memory of his mother, Mrs. Jennie McIver Hall, a friend of the Jackson family.

2. China platter and six matching soup plates, which were the Jacksons'. Given by Mr. and Mrs. Sheffield Clark, Jr., in memory of Mrs. Sheffield Clark, Sr.

3. Brass dinner gong.

3A. Pottery pitcher, given by Wylie B. Ewing, of Delray, Fla. Made for a dinner given in honor of Jackson, June 11, 1834, in Wheeling, W. Va.

SHELVES No. 2 AND No. 3:

4. Forty-three pieces of gold and white china, used at the White House during Jackson's administration.

5. Pieces of buff and gold china used constantly in the White House. From a set of 600 pieces, which was given to Mrs. Rachel Jackson Lawrence when she was married.

6. Cup, saucer, plate, fork and spoon used by two Presidents, Franklin D. Roosevelt on his visit to the Hermitage, Nov. 17, 1934, and Lyndon B. Johnson on his visit here to commemorate the 200th Birthday of Andrew Jackson, March 15, 1967.

7. Six silver tablespoons of the Jacksons, loaned by Vanderbilt University.

SHELF No. 4:

8. Silver basket.

9. Some of the valuable Jackson-Decatur silver which were 8 round and oval dishes purchased by Jackson from the widow

of Commodore Decatur, and used constantly for years at the Hermitage. (See letter regarding the purchase in Document Standard in Case B.)

10. Jackson's memorandum to his secretary regarding the purchase of the Decatur silver.

11. Salad fork and spoon, which were presented by Mrs. Andrew Jackson, Jr., to Miss Sarah Livingston on the occasion of her marriage to Judge Beard, at Tulip Grove, and were presented to The Ladies' Hermitage Association by her daughters, Mrs. Thos. Pierce of St. Louis, Mrs. Beverly R. McKennie, and Mrs. Weaver Harris.

11A. Silver compote, one of the pieces of the Decatur silver.

12. Old English silver coffee pot on trivet, presented to Wm. H. Calhoun, Nashville, in 1848 by Andrew Jackson, Jr. These pieces were in daily use during General Jackson's residence at the White House. Loaned by Vanderbilt University.

12A. Pieces of flat silver in daily use at the Hermitage.

13. Silver sugar tongs.

14. Silver muffineer or sugar shaker.

15. Pair of silver napkin rings.

16. Silver cups, marked A. J. and R. J., in daily use by General and Mrs. Jackson.

17. General Jackson's communion cup.

18. China cup, out of which General Jackson drank on the day of his death, and spoon used daily.

18A. A buff and gold china tea cup and saucer, given to Mrs. C.A.R. Thompson by Rachel Jackson Lawrence. Presented to the Hermitage by the heirs of Miss Annie Kenneth Thompson.

19. China cup and saucer, of Louis Philippe, purchased by Jackson from his steward, Boulanger. Obtained from the McIver family.

19A. Silver coffee pot given by Miss Clarissa Wentworth Collins of Montclair, N. J.

20. Original blue plate, one of set of china used by General Jackson at the Hermitage. (English reproductions of this plate are sold in the Souvenir Shop.)

SHELF No. 5:

22. A pair of coasters with glass decanters.

23. Salt cellar.

24. Caster with glass bottles.

25. Silver nut crackers and picks.

26. Wine cart on wheels (mate in dining room).

27. Wine glass used by President Jackson at the White House, 1829-1837. Given by Bettie Hoffstetter Reise.

27A. Hock or wine glass, used at the dinner in honor of Lafayette. Given by a member of the Jackson family to Mrs. W. L. Granbery, a friend and neighbor at Tulip Grove, the adjoining plantation. Presented to the Association by Mr. and Mrs. J. T. Granbery.

28. Bohemian decanter.

29. Cut glass used at the White House during Jackson's administration, including a decanter, eight wine glasses, five tumblers.

30. Silver and cut glass pickle jar.

31. Pair of Jacksonion glass decanters, presented by Mrs. Lyndon B. Johnson on the occasion of her visit to the Hermitage. to commemorate the 200th Birthday of Andrew Jackson March 15, 1967.

Case No. 4

SHELF NO. 1:

1. Letter from President Jackson to Major Andrew J. Donelson, Louisville, 1837.

2. Communication of John Quincy Adams, 1819, to John Rodgers, President of the Navy Board.

3. Letters of General Jackson, May 24, 1833.

4. Letter from Thos. Jordan, requesting appointment as Revenue Agent for the State of Maine, initialed "A. J." with memorandum.

5. Letter from Columbus, Ohio, supporters of Jackson, December 12, 1832, with notation in Jackson's handwriting.

6. Communication from Andrew Jackson to the U. S. Senate, nominating members of his Cabinet: "Edward Livingston of Louisiana, Secretary of State; Lewis McLane, of Delaware, Secretary of the Treasury; Lewis Cass, of Michigan, Secretary of War; Levi Woodbury, of New Hampshire, Secretary of the Navy; R. B. Taney, of Maryland, Attorney General of the United States." Dated, December 7, 1831.

SHELF NO. 2:

7 "The Jackson Wreath," published 1829, includes an interesting account of the last hours and death of Rachel Jackson. Presented by Mrs. James A. Wemyss, of Gallatin, who inherited it from her great-grandfather, John Branch, Secretary of the Navy in Jackson's first cabinet.

7A. Invitation from General Jackson to his neighbors, Dr. and Mrs. Doyle, Fountain of Health, to dine at the Hermitage, Dec. 26, 1840. Presented by Miss Decatur J. Page, descendant of the Doyles. Copy of the Globe, Dec. 5, 1837, inscribed "Jackson, Fountain of Health" which was the nearest post office. Given by Mrs. Lee Hunt.

8. Rare copy of the first inaugural address (1828) of President Andrew Jackson. Printed on satin, in original frame, including blown glass cover. Presented by Amon C. Evans of Nashville.

9. Inaugural address of General Andrew Jackson, March 4, 1833.

9A. Photocopy of resolution nominating President Jackson to the New York Society of the Cincinnati.

10. Invitation to the Eighth of January Ball, 1831, Nashville, issued to Miss Clementine Boyd.

10A. Jackson's Nullification Proclamation.

10B. Letter from Emperor of San Domingo to Commodore Elliott, September 6, 1832, with notation by Jackson.

10C. Letter from James Madison to M. Cathcart.

SHELF No. 3:

13. Jackson's message to congress upon offer of Smithsonian grant. A photo presented by James G. Stahlman of Nashville.

14. Extract from letter, signed Frederick P. Ladd, Boston, August 29, 1829, regarding Jackson's candidacy for President.

15. Letter to Andrew Jackson from N. Gevelot, Dec. 28, 1833, presenting bust of Jackson.

16. Letter regarding supplies ordered for White House, June 19, 1829.

17. The presidential announcement of Jackson's death issued by the Adjutant General's office in Washington. A gift from Mr. and Mrs. William Randolph Hearst, Jr., of New York.

18. A politician's manual, exhibiting the returns and votes for electors of President and Vice-president, in different states in 1828. Presented by Mr. and Mrs. William Randolph Hearst, Jr., of New York.

19. Gold watch presented by Andrew Jackson to Andrew Jackson Donelson, his nephew and ward upon his graduation from Cumberland College in 1816. The time piece was made about 1814 by the Brothers Melly, Swiss manufacturers of fine watches. Three keys are required to wind the watch. It was presented with its original embroidered bag by Mr. and Mrs. William Randolph Hearst, Jr., of New York.

20. An original memorandum of Jackson as President to the Secretary of State. A gift from Mr. and Mrs. William Randolph Hearst, Jr.

Case No. 5

SHELF No. 1:

1. Letter from Charleston, S. C., officials, expressing gratification over Major-General Jackson's proposed visit to the city, March 7, 1821.

2. Commodore Elliott's invitation to Martin Van Buren to visit Navy Yard.

3. Address to citizens of Connecticut by the friends of Andrew Jackson in 1828.

4. Medallions, illustrating stories from the Bible. On the reverse side is the story itself. This unique set was presented to General Jackson by an admirer.

5. Pamphlet containing refutation of charges made about Jackson's marriage by political enemies in Cincinnati, 1827.

6. Pamphlet in vindication of General Jackson regarding the executions of Arbuthnot and Ambrister, 1824.

7. Wooden statuette given by Jackson to granddaughter, Rachel, whose family gave it to the Hermitage after her death in 1923. The figures represent Louis Philippe and Jackson, saluting one another upon the payment of the indemnity due from France. The carving on the base represents the vessels bringing the gold from France; the hickory tree symbolizes the firmness of Jackson in demanding payment; the circle formed by the arms of the two symbolizes the lasting friendship between them. Carved by Pierre Joseph Landry, comrade-in-arms of General Jackson at the Battle of New Orleans; this was presumably presented to Jackson by the sculptor.

8. Pamphlet on the Battle of New Orleans.

9. Cartoon showing Jackson receiving cash payment from French cavalry March, 1836.

10. Copy of letter of Commodore Elliott, presenting the sarcophagus of Emperor Severus to General Jackson, given by the Hon. John Wesley Gaines.

11. Copy of General Jackson's letter declining the sarcophagus, presented by the Hon. John Wesley Gaines.

12. Photographs of the sarcophagus, now at the Smithsonian Institution, given by former Secretary of War, Jacob McGavock Dickinson.

13. Copy of New York *Herald* of June 25, 1845, with pictures and description of Jackson's funeral procession. Given by Mrs. James A. Wemyss, of Gallatin.

14. Jackson's first message to Congress, December 8, 1829, printed on silk. Presented by Mrs. Kendall Stickney, Monorvia, California.

Floor Case

A collection of three letters written by Andrew Jackson at the Hermitage. Presented to The Ladies' Hermitage Association by Joseph Kelley of Ellensville, N. Y.

Three account books of Andrew Jackson and his partners when he was an active merchant in Middle Tennessee.

A cancelled check signed by Andrew Jackson on the Bank of the Metropolis, Washington, D. C. on 9th April 1835. Presented by Andrew Jackson Baker, Jr., in memory of his grandfather and father who served as custodians of the Hermitage from 1895 until 1963.

North Room (Museum)

ON THE WALLS:

1. Bronze bust of General Jackson by Belle Kinney.
2. Battle of New Orleans. Presented by C. F. Gunther, of Chicago, Endicott & Co., Lithographers, published by T. Yeager Race Street, Philadelphia.
3. Print of General Jackson at New Orleans.
5. Engraving of the Hermitage. This is not correctly drawn. (Francis Strickland, Architect, Lith. of Endicott & Co., N.Y.).
6. Engraving of Jackson.
7. Picture of Jackson at the Hermitage, 1830. Given by J. McGavock Dickinson.
9. Land Grant signed by President Jackson. Given by J. McGavock Dickinson.
10. Appointment of Chas. A. Anderson as secretary to the French Court by Jackson, 1836. Presented in memory of Ewin Lamar Davis by his wife.
11. Illustrated Map of Nashville 1832.
12. Certificate of Major-General Andrew Jackson's membership in the Hibernian Society , March , 1819.
13. Three pictures of Uncle Alfred, colored servant, born 1803 and died in 1901. He lived in the log house back of the mansion and is buried in the garden next to the Jacksons' tomb. Given by Dr. Harry Vaughan and Mrs. Paul E. DeWitt.
14. Equestrian Statue of Jackson. This picture hung in President James K. Polk's room at the White House. Presented by Mrs. George William Fall.
14A. Engraving of General Jackson from a painting by Thomas Sully.
15. Death of Pakenham. Presented by C. F. Gunther, of Chicago, Endicott & Co., Lithographers, published by T. Yeager, Race Street, Philadelphia.
16. Blueprints showing the battlefield of Chalmette at New Orleans. Presented by Hon. John Wesley Gaines.
17. An early drawing of the Hermitage by Norman Marsh. Copy of print from the collection of Mrs. Samuel Heiskell, now at the University of North Carolina.
18. Engraving of Andrew Jackson,given by Mr. and Mrs. Whiteford Cole, Jr., in memory of his mother.

Case No. 1

1. Engraving of General Jackson.

2. Clothing worn by General Andrew Jackson: dressing gowns and slippers, wool socks used when riding in winter weather; night shirts, pen marked, "Andrew Jackson," and numbered in indelible ink.

3. Account books used in stores owned by Jackson—Gallatin, 1803; Hunter's Hill, 1804; Clover Bottom, 1805.

4. Picture of "Aunt Hannah," Mrs. Jackson's personal maid, who was with her at her death.

5. Writing case inscribed "Presented to Andrew Jackson, President of the U. S., from the State of New Hampshire."

6. Uncle Alfred, General Jackson's coachman and personal servant, born in 1803 lived for 98 years. His entire life was spent in service to the Jackson family and the Hermitage.

Case No. 2

British uniform (coat and waistcoat) taken at the Battle of New Orleans. Loaned by Andrew Jackson Lawrence, grandson of Andrew Jackson, Jr.

Case No. 3

Uniform and hat of Major John T. Reid, who fought with General Jackson in the Battle of New Orleans. Presented by his grandson, Mr. Maury T. Reid.

Case No. 4

SHELF No. 1:

1. Original letter of Amos Kendall, Nov. 20, 1829, and notation in Jackson's handwriting "Mr. Kendalls letter and remarks on my plans on National Bank."

2. Photograph of Mrs. Mary C. Dorris, in costume for a January 8 Ball. Mrs. Dorris was one of the four organizers of The Ladies' Hermitage Association, the first secretary and later Regent, and a life-long worker in the preservation of the Hermitage. Book, "Preservation of the Hermitage" by Mrs. Dorris (Copies may be purchased in Souvenir Shop).

3. Small Liberty Bell, made from the overflow of the Columbia Liberty Bell. These small bells were purchased by patriotic associations to be rung on patriotic occasions.

3A. Mourning badge worn at the time of the death of General Andrew Jackson.

4. Photograph of Mrs. Rachel Jackson Lawrence, Jacksons' favorite grandchild and namesake of Mrs. Jackson.

5. Photograph of Colonel Andrew Jackson, III, whose wife, Mrs. Amy Jackson, conceived the idea of the Hermitage Association and it was from this couple that most of the relics were purchased.

6. Frog doorstop, a presidental campaign piece, "I croak for the Jackson Wagon" given by Mrs. C. F. DeLap of Springfield, Tenn.

7. Bust by Zolnay of Mrs. Mary L. Baxter, first Regent of The Ladies' Hermitage Association. Also an appeal to Association members dated 1895 and signed by Mrs. Nathaniel Baxter, Regent.

8. Booklet and program on the exercises held at the presentation of Jackson's statue by the State of Tennessee to the United States Capitol, April 11, 1928. The statue, which is by Belle Kinney, stands in the Capitol Rotunda.

9. Picture of Healy, artist sent by Louis Philippe to paint Andrew Jackson and other prominent Americans.

10. Original floor plan of the Hermitage (changes in this were made during construction).

11. Souvenirs of President Theodore Roosevelt's visit in October, 1907. Special register with autograph signature.

12. Poem to Rachel Jackson Lawrence by Emma Look Scott.

12A. Copy Book of Maine Student containing interesting references to the Presidential election of 1825, given by Mrs. Henry W. Dearborn, Cape Elizabeth, Maine.

SHELF No. 2:

13. Topaz Necklace which belonged to Emily Donelson, hostess of the White House in Jacksons administration. Note case.

13A. Messages by President Andrew Jackson to U. S. Congress. Leather bound volume, printed on silk.

13B. Commemorative and regular issue Jackson and Hermitage stamps, 1863-1963. Given by Dr. Pembroke J. Hart.

13C. Rare Confederate States of America postage stamp, issued in 1863 with portrait of Andrew Jackson. Presented by John Heflin of Nashville.

13D. Early Hermitage gift shop souvenirs, presented by Mrs. Roy C. Avery of Nashville, Tenn.

14. Flag from the grave of Lafayette, procured for the Association by Miss M. E. Ford through General Horace Porter, Ambassador to France.

15. Letter written by President Jackson, 1828, to Lafayette. Presented by Reed Schermerhorn.

16. Appointment of Samuel B. Marshall as Marshal of Western District of Tennessee, April, 1831. Presented by Mrs. Joseph A. Gray.

17. Coin token with head of Jackson. Presented by Mrs. Wm. H. Dow, Portland, Maine.

18. Cane. Charles Sayers, personal friend of Jackson, cut the cane while walking on the Hermitage grounds with Jackson. Presented by Mrs. Wm. P. Delafield, Dallas, Texas.

19. Cane. Presented by H. V. S. Negus of Bound Brook, N. J. It was a present from General Jackson to Mr. Negus' grandfather, James Engle Negus, a native of Philadelphia who had visited General Jackson at the Hermitage frequently; they were close friends.

20. A cane, hand made by Major McCalla, who served with General Jackson at the Battle of New Orleans. Presented by Dr. C. A. Miller.

21. Silhouette of Andrew Jackson. Presented by Mrs. Whitefoord Cole.

23. Pictures of:
   (A) Mrs. Emily Donelson, hostess at the White House.
   (B) Mrs. Sarah York Jackson, wife of adopted son.
   (C) Mrs. Rachel Jackson Lawrence, in childhood.

25. Picture of costume worn by Mrs. Andrew Jackson, Jr., at her wedding reception in the White House, and now in the Museum of History and Technology in Washington, D. C., with costumes of other mistresses of the White House.

26. Centennial medal, Jackson, Michigan, designed and presented by James B. Field of Jackson, Michigan, in honor of General Jackson.

26A. Gold earrings which belonged to Nancy Gill, a collateral relative of Andrew Jackson. Presented by Mrs. Harry M. Bill of Philadelphia, through Mrs. Richard France and Dr. John Clark Finney, D.D. formerly of Philadelphia, now of Nashville.

27. Octagon House, Washington, D. C., where General Jackson was entertained. In a perfect state of preservation. Headquarters of the American Institute of Architects. Presented by Mrs. Cordelia Jackson, September 20, 1922.

28. Letter to Andrew Jackson written by Robert C. Foster, and presented to Mrs. Harry W. Evans, Regent, by Robert Coleman Foster, VII, great-grandson of the writer.

29. Watch given by Andrew Jackson to his ward, General Daniel Smith Donelson, upon his entry to West Point. Presented by Samuel Donelson, grandson of the original owner.

30. Home of Christopher Taylor, near Jonesboro where Andrew Jackson boarded. Presented by L. M. McCowan.

30A. Gold top cane presented by Pedro G. Salom, Jr., of Chester Springs, Pa. Note Silver Capsule that inserts in the head of the cane and parchment inscription that documents the cane.

SHELF NO. 4:

31. Photostat copies of bill from doctor attending Rachel Jackson

in her final illness and bill for her coffin, 1828. Presented by C. Norton Owen of Chicago.

32. Photostat copy of Deed of Trust for family graveyard, in Hermitage garden, to John H. Eaton, John Coffee, and Andrew Jackson, Jr. Presented by West Morton, 1926.

33. Bill of conveyance of slaves. Presented in memory of Jonas Redelsheimer.

34. Andrew Jackson (by Earl) in the capitol of Montgomery, Alabama. Presented to The Ladies' Hermitage Association by Sarah E. Cowan, great-niece of Rachel Jackson.

35. Itemized statement of Dr. McCorkle's bill to Andrew Jackson, October, 1825. Presented by Mrs. E. A. Lindsey. Of Special interest is reference to Jackson's solicitude for the health and welfare of his slaves.

36. President Jackson's contract with his cook, Prevaux. Presented by Mrs. Bettie M. Donelson.

37. Currier & Ives Print; Death bed scene of General Jackson.

38. A collection of souvenirs sold at the Hermitage in 1899. Presented by Mrs. A. M. Mergner of Bronxville, N. Y.

39. Cedar jewelry box, an early souvenir sold at the Hermitage around 1900. Presented by Mrs. Leon Spillman of Miami, Florida.

40. Hermitage souvenirs sold during the early years of the Hermitage.

Case No. 5

Clothing and personal possessions of the Jacksons:

The red velvet dress, worn by Sarah Jackson at the White House (which is the same as in the Earl portrait of her in the Hermitage dining room) was given by her great-granddaughter, Sue Rhea Symmes McCutcheon, in memory of her grandmother, Rachel Jackson Lawrence. Velvet sample shows original color. The letter was written by Andrew Jackson from the White House, 1832 to his daughter-in-law, Sarah York Jackson. The leather hat box has the following name plate: "General Andrew Jackson, President of the United States" and the hat with the ten-inch mourning band is the one he wore in Washington following the death of his wife. The rosewood cane was his favorite walking stick. Displayed with one of his suits is a linen shirt made by seamstress Gracey who lived at the Hermitage. The lavender moire dress, which was Rachel Jackson's, was presented by her great-granddaughter, Marion Lawrence Symmes, and the white shawl, said to have been hers, was given by Mrs. Bertha Pierce, of Daytona, Fla. The lace cap belonged to Rachel Jackson, and also the aquamarine necklace.

Floor Standard

A. Letters from Senator Edmond de Lafayette, grandson of General Lafayette, concerning the French chair he gave to the

Hermitage, which is in the Brides' Room.

B. Steubenville Republican Ledger, reporting supper given in honor of Jackson's triumph, Nov. 26, 1828, and Jackson's election returns, 1828.

C. Copy of National Banner and Nashville Whig, Aug. 12, 1828, given by C. L. Winn, great-grandson of Andrew Jackson, Jr. and Sarah York Jackson. Contains commendations of Jackson's policy during Creek Campaign.

D. Interesting expressions of Jackson's characteristics of spirituality and patriotism in a letter (January 8, 1822) to his ward, E. G. W. Butler, purchased from his grandson, E. G. Butler.

E. Signed military orders from various officers, 1814.

F. Pay-rolls from Capt. Haley, Llewellyn Griffith and Major H. D. Peire.

G. Military orders signed by Jackson and muster roll of regiment commanded by Stockly Donelson, 1792. Extracts from letters of Capt. Thos. Preston, John Overton, and J. Winchester and receipts signed by Jackson.

H. Letter from Jackson to Dr. John L. Wynn. Photostat letter from Rachel Jackson to her brother, Capt. John Donelson, Aug. 25, 1821.

I. Note of presentation of plaster cast of Powers bust, from Levi Woodbury and Jackson's reply. Letter from Jackson to Sarah York Jackson, April 14, 1835.

J. Letter of condolence from Rachel Jackson to her niece, Catherine Caffery Walker, on the death of her sister, Jane Caffery Earl. A letter from Andrew Jackson to Catherine Caffery Walker, regarding business matters, presented by a descendant, Vera Walker Morel.

K. Letter from D. Morrison, contractor, concerning additions to the house and erection of the tomb.
Letter from Jackson to A. J. Donelson, presented by Mrs. P. H. Manlove.

L. West Carolinian Extra Dec. 7, 1833, containing Jackson's message to Congress. This paper, which originally belonged to Jackson's law instructor, Judge Spruce Macay, was given by Mrs. Fannie McNeely of Salisbury, N. C.

Wall Standard

CASE A:

Jackson's appointment as Judge of Superior Court, signed by John Sevier, December 22, 1798.

Jackson's receipt from post office, June 2, 1826, for payment on his 17 newspaper subscriptions.

Invitation to Military Ball given at Huntsville Inn, 1825, in commemoration of the Battle of New Orleans. Presented by Mrs. George Dury, to whose grandmother the invitation was issued.

Photostatic copy of statement by Dr. Catlet regarding Dickinson duel.

Letter from Jackson to Judge John Overton, regarding the former's "conduct in Florida" and Eaton's appeal. September 16, 1831.

CASE B:

Letter describing White House reception for Andrew Jackson, Jr., and his bride, from Emily Donelson, Washington, 1831.

Note from Jackson to his wife, February 6, 1804.

Letter from Mrs. Stephen Decatur regarding sale of silver and china -and Jackson's signed receipt of his purchases.

General Jackson's orders for medicine and hospital stores, Nov. 4, 1813.

CASE C:

Photostatic copy of letter regarding birthplace of Jackson and burial place of his mother and father, from James H. Witherspoon, Lancaster, S. C., April 16, 1825.

Land grant, signed by Jackson, presented by Mrs. J. C. Cartwright.

Letter from Dr. Beaumont to Jackson expressing solicitude for latter's health and presenting his book on medicine.

Photostat of Major General Jackson's orders to his troops, Nov. 24, 1812.

Election returns from Globe Extra, November 15, 1832. Presented by Judge John H. DeHitt.

CASE D:

Letter from Jackson to Maj. A. J. Donelson, 1837, relating the ovations he received en route from Washington to Nashville.

Letter from Jackson to Maj. A. J. Donelson, July 25, 1833, giving instructions for Hermitage farming operations and requesting him to check and report on them.

Official nomination of John H. Baker as Secretary of French Treaty Commission notation by Jackson.

Letter to Jackson from Roger B. Taney, Attorney General, regarding New Orleans banks.

Case E:

Letter in French regarding Louisiana colonies.

Ship passport, signed by Jackson, June 4, 1835.

Letter accompanying original Treasury Draft, remitting the famous Judge Hall fine.

Case F:

Photostatic copies of bills and letters from Philadelphia dealers regarding Hermitage furnishings purchased in 1837 and of bills for remodeling mansion after the fire in 1834.

Case G:

Copies of bills for Hermitage furnishings purchased in 1837.

Letter from Jane Caffrey, Hermitage, Feb. 1815, regarding the Battle of New Orleans, presented by Vera Walker Morel.

Poem written on Jackson's birthday, March 15, 1837, White House.

Letters to Major A. J. Donelson, telling of marauder's attempt to break in to President Jackson's bedroom.

Case H:

Letter from Jackson to his neighbor Dr. Doyle, requesting his consulation with Col. Jeremiah George Harris' physicians at the time of his accident.

Letter from Lord Byron, Venice, 1819, to his Paris publishers, remonstrating against publishing under his name volumes of which he was not the author. Presented by Earl to Jackson, along with volume of Byron's poems.

Case I:

Letter from Jackson to Maj. Wm. B. Lewis, February 28, 1845, regarding Polk's cabinet and other political matters.

Letter to President Jackson from Edward Livingston, Paris, May 6, 1834.

A photo copy of the result of the apportionment of the real property of the deceased Severn Donelson.

Case J:

Letter from Andrew Jackson to Major William B. Lewis, Aug. 6 1814, referring to military matters.

Letter from Andrew Jackson to Dr. Doyle, Fountain of Health, requesting bill for services to his ward, Dec. 27, 1840.

Letter, Andrew Jackson to Andrew Jackson, Jr.

THE MANSION

The Hermitage is built in southern colonial style of architecture, with large verandas in front and rear, a wide hallway, with two rooms on either side, and wings supplementing these. The rooms are spacious, and are eleven in number, besides pantry, storeroom, kitchen, cellar. There is a smoke-house and other outhouses. In 1922 a steam furnace was installed at a safe distance from the mansion, eliminating danger of fire from this source.

The Hall

The hall contains the original hat rack, umbrella stand, two mahogany sofas, pier table, Brussels stair carpet and brass rods, and the chandelier. The hall floor originally was covered with oilcloth. The pictorial wallpaper was printed by duFour in Paris, about 1825. The complete set consisted of twenty-five strips in colors, and was ordered by General Jackson in 1835, being the original paper used when the house was rebuilt. It was shipped by way of New Orleans up the Mississippi and Cumberland Rivers. This paper is of outstanding historical interest, one of the few historic, scenic papers preserved in this country.

The paper represents the legend of the travels of Telemachus in search of Ulysses, his father, and is that part of the story of his landing on the island of Calypso. He is accompanied by Mentor.

SCENE I. The landing and the Queen advancing to meet them.

SCENE II. Telemachus relating the story of his travels to Calypso, the faithful Mentor by his side.

SCENE III. Calypso gives a fete in his honor, and Cupid begins to play a part.

SCENE IV. Telemachus resolves to escape; Calypso's maidens burn his boat, and he jumps from the cliffs.

In October, 1930, the paper was removed from the walls by Mr. James Wilson from the Metropolitan Museum in New York, for the purpose of treating the walls to insure the preservation of the paper, and was then put back.

1. Brass candlestick, presented by Mrs. Percy Warner.

2. Glass celande or hurricane shade.

The Front Parlor

All the furnishings in this room are originals. The chandelier, the Parian marble vase and French china vase on wall brackets, the gold mirror, the mantel of Italian marble, mirror over mantel, the Japanese bronze clock inlaid with enamel, the matching candelabra, the two mahogany carved chairs, marble top table, portfolio and autograph album (inlaid with mother-of-pearl, containing two signatures of Sam Houston and presented by Mr. and Mrs. Richard Plater), Bohemian glass dish, mahogany whatnot, brass cup, large mahogany sofa, carpet and pier table are all pieces used when the Jacksons were living in the Hermitage. The lace curtains are exact reproductions of the original ones, made by Salmon Freres of Paris, France. The original red brocatel draperies were replaced in 1954 with exact reproductions of the fabric, made by Scalamandre Silks, which fabric was also used to replace the uphostering on the red chairs and the matching draperies in the back parlor. (Part of the original curtains and draperies displayed in the museum.)

1. Two carved chairs presented to Jackson by the Khedive of Egypt, when Jackson was President.
2. Portrait of General Jackson presented by Mrs. Thomas M. Steger.
3. Portrait of Mrs. Jackson in ball dress.
5. Pair of French vases.
6. Bronze andirons, representing the Vestal Virgin.
7. Portrait of Andrew Jackson by Healy, the artist who was commissioned by Louis Philippe to paint the portrait, only two of which are in existence. The other one hangs in the Louvre, Paris, painted eight days before Jackson's death. See Healy letter in Museum.
8. Opal vases presented by Andrew and Albert Marble Jackson.
9. Two liqueur bottles, presented by Lafayette to General Jackson.
10. One of a pair of brass lamps with crystal prisms used at the Hermitage by the Jackson family. Purchased from the heirs of Samuel Jackson Lawrence by The Ladies' Hermitage Association. Duplicate in BACK PARLOR.
11. Silver filigree basket.
12. Chair used in the White House during President Jackson's administration. Presented by Miss Laura Friesbee of Washington, D. C.
13. Portrait of General Jackson by R. E. W. Earl, given by Mr. and Mrs. William Randolph Hearst, Jr.

Back Parlor

All furnishings in this room are also originals (except lace curtains and draperies). The chandelier, pier table, mahogany chair, two chairs and tilt top table with mother-of-pearl inlay, mahogany card table, two velvet chairs, Parian marble and

French china vase on wall brackets, brass andirons and fender, gold oval mirror, pair of silver girandoles beaded mat and brass candlestick are all pieces used at the Hermitage by the Jacksons. The mantle is of Tennessee marble.

15. Sewing box inlaid with mother-of-pearl belonged to Mrs. Andrew Jackson; Mrs. Jackson presented it to Mrs. Emily Donelson; Mrs. Donelson gave it to Mrs. Wilcox (her daughter); Mrs. Wilcox gave it to Mrs. Andrew Price; through Mr. and Mrs. Richard Plater it was presented to The Ladies' Hermitage Association.

16. Portrait of General Coffee.

17. Portrait of General Bronaugh.

18. Portrait of Colonel Gadsden.

19. Portrait of Lieutenant Eastland.

    (These four constituted the Staff Officers generally called "General Jackson's military family.")

20. Clock, one of the oldest relics, in the Hermitage before the death of Mrs. Rachel Jackson. The hands are set at the hour Jackson died.

21. Pair of Girandoles used in the White House while Jackson was President.

22. Jackson piano presented by Colonel Andrew Jackson, grandson of Andrew Jackson.

23. Music book belonging to Mrs. Emily Donelson, First Lady of the White House. Presented by Mrs. Bettie M. Donelson.

24. Two gilt wall brackets bought by Andrew Jackson, Jr.

25. Flower jar presented by Andrew Jackson, IV, and Albert Marble Jackson (on wall bracket). Duplicate in front parlor.

26. Mirror willed to the Association by Mrs. Alice Watkins Shields of Knoxville in 1934, originally at the Hermitage.

27. Nut bowls, and compote (on pier table).

28. Guitar of Mrs. Sara York Jackson, presented by the Rev. Walton Lawrence Smith, a descendant.

29. Mahogany center table. The only piece remaining of the set presented to General and Mrs. Jackson when on a visit to New Orleans after the battle. The gold spectacles on the table were worn by Mrs. Jackson and the volume of Robert Burns' poems is inscribed, "Rachel Jackson from her beloved husband, Andrew Jackson."

30. Mahogany sofa bought by Mrs. Hoffstetter at the sale of the adopted son's effects in 1866. Presented to the Association in 1897 by Miss Bettie Hoffstetter of Nashville.

31. Pair of silver lustre vases sent to General Jackson from the Czar of Russia.

General Jackson's Bedroom

This room is as it was the day he died, with the same furniture he used, the bed he died upon, the chair he sat in, etc. The furnishings consist of bedstead, bureau, wardrobe, washstand with china pieces, table, chair, settee or sofa, wallpaper, bedspread, andirons and fender, mirror, etc. The same pictures are on the wall. The bedspread is a replica of the original, handmade with the initials R. J. embroidered on it. The original is in the Museum. The bed and window draperies are exact reproductions of those used in the winter during Jackson's lifetime, having been made by Scalamandre Silks, Inc., in New York, N. Y. Part of the original fabric is in the Museum.

1. Portrait of his wife by Earl, over the mantle, upon which his dying gaze rested.
2. Portrait of the adopted son, Andrew Jackson, Jr., in childhood, by Earl.
3. Earl portrait of the granddaughter, Mrs. Rachel J. Lawrence (eldest child of the adopted son), the pet and companion of his declining years.
3A. French china teapot or veilleuse, with place for light at bottom, sometimes used as night. light. This relic of General Jackson was sold by descendants to the McIver family. The Association purchased it in 1959 from Miss Effie McIver, in memory of Miss Felicia Grundy Porter.
4. Chinese Mandarin scent bottles. Belonged to Mrs. Jackson.
5. Shell jewel case, which was Mrs. Jackson's.
6. Portrait of Jackson.
7. Shell vases on mantel, which belonged to Mrs. Jackson.
8. Steel engraving, the "Sixth Seal." This is an illustration of The Revelation, Chapter 6:12, 17, engraved by G. H. Phillips from the original picture by F. Danby, A. R. A., in collection of Wm. Beckford, Esq.
9. Colored print, "Battle of the Thames."
10. Colored print, "Battle of North Point."
11. Tobacco box, used by the General.
12. His leather hatbox.
13. Original hair brush and clothes brush, strawberry design on back.
14. Picture of Judge John Overton, bearing his signature. Judge Overton was Jackson's law partner and lifelong friend.

Andrew Jackson, Jr.'s Bedroom

This was General and Mrs. Jackson's room previous to the death of Mrs. Jackson in 1828, afterwards the bedroom of Mr. and Mrs.

Andrew Jackson, Jr. The furniture was purchased by Jackson after the fire in 1834.

The mahogany bedstead, one of eight purchased after the fire of 1834, the mahogany bureau with toilet articles, mahogany washstand with original washstand set, mahogany marble top center table, triple mirror, brass andirons, cut glass oil lamp. The carpet is not original, but an old one of the period. The portrait of Sarah York Jackson was painted by Healy. The leather chair was one used contantly by her. The coverlet on the bed, done in traponca needlcraft was presented by Mrs. Walter B. Smith in memory of her grandmother, Mary Phares-Bevill, who made it in 1838.

The wallpaper is a reproduction, presented by the Robert Graves Company of New York and copyrighted (1925). The wood blocks from which the paper was made were purchased by the Association.

Candlesticks on mantel, presented by Mrs. Anne Hoyte Hicks Joyce, were purchased by her grandmother, Mrs. Maggie L. Hicks, at an early auction, used by General Jackson at the Hermitage.

Bohemian glass jar, which belonged to Rachel Jackson. Presented by Mrs. W. T. Mallison.

Andrew Jackson's signature is on fly leaf of open volume, History of England, 1793.

Side Hall

1. Famous military portrait (by Earl).
2. Secretary presented to General Jackson.
3. Original sofa purchased by the Association in 1937.
4. The wallpaper in the side hall is a copy of the original.
5. Marble bust of General Jackson, presented by Hon. Lawrence Cooper, of Huntsville, Ala.
6. Precepts, given to Jackson in his early youth by his mother, which he said ruled his life. This copy presented by E. A. Lindsey and Reau E. Folk.
7. Jackson's Masonic apron loaned by Stanley F. Horn.
8. Copy of Jackson's portrait, which hangs in the Nashville Masonic Temple, the original having been painted when Jackson was Grand Master. Presented by the Grand Lodge of Free and Accepted Masons of Tennessee.
9. Presentation copy of Masonic manual, dedicated to Jackson and presented to him by the author, Wilkins Tannehill.
10. Earl portrait of Jackson, showing in the background the Hermitage as it was before it was remodeled in 1831 and preceding the fire of 1834. It was presented by Mrs. Charles W. Frear, of Troy, N. Y., in memory of her husband, who owned it for many years.

11. Jackson portrait by Sully. Presented in 1958 by Mrs. John Valentine Mershon of Philadelphia, whose grandfather, Jonathan Paul Worrall, was one of the group who originally proposed Jackson's nomination for the presidency, and who previously owned the portrait. It was carried at the head of political parades.

Office or Library

For thirty years the Hermitage was the political center of the United States, and Andrew Jackson was the most influential man of his party. Many visitors, political and otherwise, were constantly being received by General Jackson in this office.

The books are those that constituted General and Mrs. Jackson's library and some of those of the two succeeding generations. The bookcases, which were General and Mrs. Jackson's, hold volumes of history, poetry, fiction, theology, military regulations, law, medical practices for the home, veterinary science, gardening, bound state papers and newspapers of the time, school books, etc., numbering over 400.

The tables of mahogany, the brass candlestick, mahogany chairs, cut glass celande or hurricane shade, brass spittoon, boar paperweight, and owl inkstand are all original. The carpet, not originally in the Hermitage, was obtained from the home of Mrs. Edgar Foster, which was built in the period of the Hermitage. Other original furnishings are:

1. Four cherry bookcases.
2. Chair, made from wood of the frigate Constitution, presented to Levi Woodbury, Secretary of the Navy, 1837; Secretary of the Treasury, 1834, to March, 1837; during the administration of President Jackson. Presented to the Hermitage by Miss Ellen C. Woodbury, daughter of Levi Woodbury, in 1900.
3. Mahogany bookcase and desk.
4. Bust of Andrew Jackson by Luigi Persico, an Italian Sculpturer who did Columbus statue and sculptures for the east tympanum at the National Capitol.
5. and 6. Pair of paintings of DeSoto and his wife, Isabella. Presented by Louis Philippe to President Jackson.
7. Jackson's bound copies of the *Globe Democrat*, published at Washington, D. C., while he was President of the United States. Presented by Mrs. Bettie M. Donelson.
8. Old newspapers of Jackson's time (bound). Presented by Mrs. Rachel Jackson Lawrence. Atlas with Andrew Jackson's signature Sept. 12, 1835.

9. Bust of Levi Woodbury, of General Jackson's cabinet.

10. Case, made of historic wood taken from the old building first used as a statehouse in Nashville, 1812-1815. The case was made to protect the bound volumes of newspapers of Jackson's day. Wood given by Mrs. Jennie C. Buntin.

11. Invalid chair, presented to General Jackson by the Mechanics of Nashville. Invented by Dr. Holmes of South Carolina, who presented duplicates to Queen Victoria and John C. Calhoun.

12. Mahogany candlestand, upon which General Jackson always opened his mail, and candlestick on beaded mat; his Bible and spectacles.

13. Marble-topped table at which General Jackson issued directives at the Battle of New Orleans. Presented by Judge John Minnick Williams of Altus, Okla., formerly of Nashville.

14. Chair, presented to Jackson by Chief Justice Roger B. Taney.

15. Portrait by Earl of General Jackson on Sam Patch, white horse presented him in 1833 by the citizens of Pennsylvania. General Jackson rode this horse in a civic and military parade given in his honor in Philadelphia, after which it was sent to Nashville. Federal soldiers whom General Geo. H. Thomas had placed as guard at the Hermitage fired a military salute over the grave of the horse.

16. The walnut office desk with a number of secret drawers; used constantly when Jackson was practicing attorney.

17. Steel engraving of George Washington.

18. Bust of Lewis Cass, Secretary of War and Minister Plenipotentiary to France under General Jackson.

19. Liquor Chest of General Jackson. Presented by Mrs. Michael Mullens of Baltimore, Maryland.

The Nursery

This room, used until 1955 as the museum for relics and papers, was at one time during the residence of the Jacksons the overseer's room, at another the nursery.

The cherry cradle was made at the Hermitage for Andrew Jackson, Jr., and was purchased by the Association from a member of the family. The quilt on the cradle was made by Mrs. W. L. Nichol, neighbor and friend of the Jacksons, for her daughter, Julia Nichol More. Coverlet, given by Mrs. Minos Fletcher, Jr., and Paul Shwab. The bed and the rug are types used in that period. The chair, which was given by Mrs. D. W. Cantrell, belonged to a member of the Jackson family. The chest of drawers and the washstand were part of the original Hermitage furnishings, and the china toilet set, of the Jackson period, was presented by Mrs. Edgar Foster. The clock and the unique china candlesticks were also part of the Hermitage furnishings, and the thermometer was General Jackson's.

The silver cup was presented by Martin Van Buren to his godson, Andrew Jackson, III, on the occasion of his christening at the White House. The portrait over the mantel, which was at the White House and also hung in the Hermitage nursery, is of the twin children of Marcus Talmage, of New York, namesakes of Andrew and Rachel Jackson. Presented by the Talmages. The French doll of 1830 was given to the Hermitage by the Dixie-Dollers Club.

The wooden hat box, which belonged to Jackson's mother, Elizabeth Hutchinson Jackson, was given by Mrs. Clara Hudgins Cowgill. The print of General Jackson is by Currier and Ives. One of the pictures is of Mrs. Lucius Polk and her son, William. As Mary Eastin, she spent much time at the White House with the Jacksons during her young ladyhood and was married there. The other picture is of Mary Eastin and Madame Pageot (daughter of Jackson's close friend, Maj. Wm. B. Lewis) who was also one of the Jacksons' favorites and was married there. Both pictures, made from portraits owned by the family of Mrs. Lucius E. Burch, were presented by Mrs. Burch. The small oil painting by the ten-year-old daughter of Peter G. Washington was a gift to Jackson during his presidency.

THE UPPER CHAMBERS

Earl's Room

Ralph E. W. Earl, son of the distinguished artist, Ralph Earl, was a member of the Hermitage and White House households for 20 years. He married Jane Caffery, niece of Mrs. Jackson, who died within a year and Earl never remarried. He painted numerous fine portraits of Jackson and other notables. He is buried in the Hermitage garden, the gravestone being inscribed, "Erected in memory of Col. R. E. W. Earl, Friend and Companion of General Andrew Jackson, who died at the Hermitage, Sept. 16, 1838."

The bed, the chest, the mirror, the chair of Venetian ironwork, used as a barber's chair, all belonged to the original furnishings. The wallpaper is also the original. The carpet which is of the same period was presented by Mrs. Horatio Berry. A quilt of the period is the gift of Mrs. Louise Blackwell, of Warrenton, Va.

1. Portrait of Col. Jeremiah George Harris. Purser of the Navy, Editor of National Union and close friend of Jackson. Presented by his daughter, Mrs. Van S. Lindsley.
2. Portrait of Jackson by Earl.

3. Pair of shell letter racks presented to Mrs. Jackson in 1827 (letter of presentation in the Museum.)
4. Banjo owned by President Jackson, loaned by Miss Emma Hoffstetter.
5. French whatnot, a gift from Louis Philippe of France.

Little Rachel's Room

First child of the adopted son, Andrew Jackson, Jr., and Sarah York Jackson, "Little Rachel" was born at the Hermitage. She was always the special pet of Jackson and was one of those who stood by his bedside when he died. This room was refurnished for her with these rosewood pieces when she married Dr. J. M. Lawrence in 1852. The table belonged to Jackson. The wall paper is original, but the carpet is one of the period. The quilt was made by "Little Rachel" and was presented by Mrs. R. H. Oliphant, of San Mateo, Calif., in memory of her mother. The portrait over the mantel of Rachel Jackson Lawrence in her later years was presented by her family. She is pictured wearing the miniature of her grandmother Jackson, for whom she was named, and which was given to her by President Jackson with the injunction never to go without it. A portrait of Andrew Jackson by the artist Wood, acquired by the Association in 1910. Washstand set of the period, given by Mrs. David P. Adams.

The bronze lamp on mantel was among the original Hermitage furnishings.

The Upper Hall

1. Jackson's old cedar chest.
2. Steel engraving "Sortie on Gibraltar."
3. Steel engraving, "Siege of Gibraltar."
4. Steel engraving of Jackson on Sam Patch, willed to the Association by Miss Elizabeth Archer.
5. Oration on General Jackson, delivered by George Bancroft, U. S. Secretary of the Navy, in Washington, June 27, 1845 (one of 24 public eulogies delivered by various national leaders following Jackson's death).

Guest Room

It was the Hermitage custom to welcome all travelers; this room was one used to accommodate some of the numerous guests. The two mahogany beds are original. The Association possesses six of the eight mahogany beds purchased when the house was refurnished in 1835. Also among the original furnishings are the cedar chest, mahogany washstand and wardrobe, the mirror, a pair of Dresden vases, the mother-of-pearl inlay plate, the small leather trunk and the hatbox, and the wallpaper is original. The bowl and pitcher, presented by Mary Felice Ferrell, were given to her grandfather by Jackson. The Venetian ironwork chair was used as a barber's chair. The carpet is an old one of the period.

1. Portrait of Jackson by Earl.
2. Portrait of Jackson by an unknown artist.

The Brides' Room

As General and Mrs. Jackson were greatly beloved by the younger members of her family and of their friends, many came, including Henry A. Wise (later Governor of Virginia) and his bride, to spend their honeymoons at the Hermitage. The guest room, therefore, was known as the Brides' Room. The mahogany bed, French dresser, wardrobe, chest and shaving stand, table, mirror and china vases were all among the original furnishings. The bedspread is handwoven, the silk quilt was made by Mrs. Julia Nichol More, granddaughter of Josiah Nichol, friend and neighbor of the Jacksons. The carpet was a gift from Miss Myrtle Drane, of Clarksville, who inherited it from her grandfather.

1. Portrait of Mrs. Jackson. Presented to the Association by Mrs. Ellen Call Long, whose father, General Call, eloped with Miss Mary Kirkman and was married at the Hermitage. This portrait and also one of General Jackson, were given to the young couple as a bridal present.
2. Chair from the Chateau de Lafayette, presented to the Association in 1890 by Senator Edmond de Lafayette, the grandson of General Lafayette. Senator Lafayette's letter in relation to this gift is in the Museum.
3. Masonic Lodge candlestick used in Gallatin by General Jackson. Presented by Col. Thomas H. Boyers.
4. Portrait of Jackson presented to the Association by Mr. and Mrs. David C. Mosby, San Francisco, Calif.

The Dining Room

Rachel Jackson's Blessing was: "Sanctify, O Lord, we beseech Thee, this provision for our good and us to Thy service for Christ's sake, Amen."

The dining room contains the original sideboard, table, some of the chairs, side table, pier table, sugar chest, andirons, and some of the silver and glass. The drapery fabric is an exact reproduction of an old brocatel pattern, by Scalamandre Silks; the carpet is one of the period. The floor is the only one in the mansion that has had to be replaced; a piece of the original flooring is in the Museum.

Adjoining the dining room is the pantry and farther to the rear the storeroom. A passageway leads directly from the dining room to the porch connecting with the kitchen.

All articles in the dining room are originals unless otherwise specified.

1. The "Old Hickory" or January 8 mantel, made of bits of hickory bark worked on only on the 8th of January of successive years, by one of Jackson's soldiers in the Battle of New Orleans. Presented to General Jackson January 8, 1839 and placed in the dining room by General Jackson, January 8, 1840.

2. Pair of bronze oil lamps.

3. The original dining table, at which several Presidents have dined: James Monroe, Martin Van Buren, James K. Polk, Theodore Roosevelt, Franklin D. Roosevelt, and Lyndon B. Johnson. Presidents Millard Fillmore, Franklin Pierce, James Buchanan, Rutherford B. Hayes, and William H. Taft, General Sam Houston, and the Marquis de Lafayette were also among the distinguished guests who have been entertained at the Hermitage.

4. Silver tray given to Jackson by Sam Houston. Presented to the Association by Mrs. Alice Watkins Shields. The large coffee pot with the initials A. J., once owned by Jackson, was returned by its recent owner, Mrs. John MacVeagh, Santa Barbara, Calif.; the three other pieces are Hermitage originals.

5. Candelabra with "wind glasses."

6. Epergne.

7. Silver wine cart. Mate in Museum.

8. Two of the Decatur silver vegetable dishes.

9. Silver egg and toast rack. Presented by Mr. and Mrs. T. Graham Hall in memory of his mother, Mrs. Jennie McIver Hall, to whose family these were given by the Jacksons.

10. Cruet set.

11. Silver covered dishes, part of the silver pieces purchased by Jackson from the widow of Commodore Decatur. The silver originally included sixteen round and oval dishes, which were used constantly for years at the Hermitage.

12. Silver candelabrum, one of a pair used at the White House, given by Miss Mary R. Wilcox.

13. Additional pieces of the Decatur silver.

14. Bohemian wine decanters and silver holders.

15. Silver wine cooler.

16. Portrait of the adopted son, Andrew Jackson, Jr. by Earl.

17. Portrait of Sarah York Jackson (wife of Andrew Jackson, Jr.). The dress in which she is pictured is in the Museum.

18. Portrait of Rachel Jackson, wife of Andrew Jackson.
19. Portrait of Andrew Jackson, about 1820.
20. Oil painting of Christopher Columbus. Presented to Jackson by S. D. Bradford of West Roxbury, Mass.
21. Portrait of General Coffee.
22. Portrait of Mary Donelson Coffee, wife of General Coffee, daughter of John Donelson and niece of Rachel Jackson. These portraits were presented by Hon. Alexander Donelson Coffee, son of General and Mrs. Coffee.

Kitchen

The restoration of the furnishings of the old kitchen to its old-time glory of yawning chimney piece, its crane and pothook, its ovens and skillets, its candle molds and spinning wheels, brings back reminiscences of the cook, "Betty," and the old regime of Jackson's day. The large stone hearth is as it was in General Jackson's day.

Spinning wheel and reel, over 100 years old. Presented by Andrew Jackson Baker, former custodian, who was born at the Hermitage.

Table of the period, given by Mrs. W. H. Wemyss.

Candle molds. Presented by Miss Louise Baxter, Mrs. W. J. McMurray, Mrs. M. A. Spurr, and Mrs. George L. Cowan.

Pothooks and Flax Hacker. Used in Revolutionary days. Presented by Miss Louise Baxter and Miss Louise G. Lindsley.

Some of the original kitchen utensils. Presented by Mrs. Andrew Jackson, III.

Copper kettle belonged to Mrs. Andrew Jackson.

Old grease lamp, given by Mrs. W. A. Hargis.

Original water cooler. Always used in the pantry.

Brass kettle. Presented by Mrs. Whitefoord Cole.

Original churn of Jackson's. Loaned by Miss Emma Hoffstetter.

Six dish covers, pair of tongs of Major Andrew Jackson Donelson's. Presented by Mrs. Bettie M. Donelson.

Original old wafer irons. Presented by Mrs. L. D. Hill and Mrs. John K. Maddin.

Original kitchen "safe," for keeping food.

Pie tins and custard cups, used by Aunt Betty, the cook.

Original spice jars, bought from China.

Original flour and meal chest.

Original brass kettles, used for preserving.

Plate given by Mary Hook, once used at the Hermitage.

Iron spit, given by Mary Felice Ferrell.

Mortar and pestle, three white platers, copper bucket, three chairs, and wood chest for table silver, used at the Hermitage.

The bells overhead on the back porch were rung from the parlor and front door.

The Old Smokehouse

A remnant of days long gone by, when the smokehouse was the most important house on a plantation. Built in 1831.

Original trough for salting meat made from one log, presented by Mrs. Cleves Symmes, granddaughter of Jackson's adopted son.

The iron kettle, used for rendering lard, was given by Mrs. E. W. Graham, great-great-grandniece of Rachel Jackson. The imitation hams show how they were hung from the beams.

A normal supply of meat for the 100 slaves, family and guests when hogs were killed was from 20,000 to 25,000 pounds.

Genuineness of the Relics

That there might never be a question raised as to the genuineness of the relics purchased, the Association has obtained from Colonel Jackson and his sister, Mrs. Rachel Jackson Lawrence, the following affidavit:

To Whom It May Concern:

This is to certify that all the articles of furniture of relics purchased by The Ladies' Hermitage Association from Mrs. Rachel Jackson Lawrence, granddaughter, and Col. Andrew Jackson, grandson of General Andrew Jackson, are the identical pieces of furniture owned and used by General Jackson during his lifetime. They were in the Hermitage when General Jackson died and were there when The Ladies' Hermitage Association took possession in 1889. The entire collection was removed in 1893, when Col. Jackson left the Hermitage, and have been restored from time to time as the Association was able to purchase them.

The articles restored up to the present time, March, 1900, are those in General Jackson's bedroom, which is complete as it was the day he died; the library, or office, entire; the hall, entire; and all furniture now in the dining room and parlors.

(SEAL)   RACHEL JACKSON LAWRENCE
                             COL. ANDREW JACKSON.

Sworn to and subscribed before me, this March 13, 1900.
                        R. S. COWAN, *Notary Public.*

Since 1900 many more pieces of the Jackson furniture and relics have been acquired and restored to the Hermitage by purchase, gift, or loan; and while it is well furnished throughout with original pieces, information is still being gathered and evaluated on some outstanding relics.

ANDREW JACKSON CHRONOLOGY

By W. B. Marr

1767	March 15	Born near the line between South Carolina and North Carolina.
1784	Fall	Began study of law.
1787	May	Admitted to practice law in North Carolina.
1788	August 12	Duel with Colonel Waightstill Avery at Jonesboro.
1788	Spring	Appointed public prosecutor for territory south of Ohio River.
1791	August	Married Mrs. Rachel Donelson Robards near Natchez, Miss.
1796	January 11	Member first constitutional convention of Tennessee.
1796		Elected representative in Congress from Tennessee.
1797	November 22	Appointed by Governor Sevier Senator from Tennessee, succeeding William Blount, resigned..
1798	June	Resigned from Senate.
1798		Elected member of the superior court of law and equity.
1801		Elected Major-General of Tennessee Militia.
1804		Moved from Hunter's Hill to log house, original Hermitage.
1804	July 24	Resigned from superior court.
1805–6		Entertained Aaron Burr.
1806	May 30	Duel with Charles Dickinson.
1809	December	Nephew of Mrs. Jackson adopted, named Andrew Jackson, Jr.
1812	June 25	Offered services of Tennessee Volunteers to the United States Government in the War of 1812.
1813	January 7	Started for New Orleans with Tennessee Militia.
1813	February 15	Arrived at Natchez.
1813	March 25	Started home from Natchez.
1813	April 22	Returned to Hermitage.
1813	September 4	Wounded in affray with Thomas H. and Jesse Benton.
1813	October 11	Started with his command for the Creek War.
1813	November 3	Battle of Talluschatches, Creek War.
1813	November 9	Battle of Talladega, Creek War.
1814	January 24	Battle of Enotocopco, Creek War.
1814	March 27	Battle of the Horseshoe, Creek War.
1814	April 19	Appointed Brigadier-General United States Army.
1814	May 1	Appointed Major-General United States Army.
1814	August 10	Had treaty with Creeks signed.
1814	September 9	Started first Florida campaign.
1814	December 2	Arrived at New Orleans for the defense of the city.
1814	December 16	Declared martial law in New Orleans.

1814	December 23	First battle in defense of New Orleans.
1815	January 1	Second battle in defense of New Orleans.
1815	January 8	Won battle of New Orleans.
1815	March 5	Caused the arrest of Judge Dominick A. Hall, United States District Judge at New Orleans.
1815	March 13	Abrogated martial law at New Orleans.
1815	March 24	Fined $1,000 by Judge Dominick A. Hall for contempt of court, which Jackson paid the same day, and which was refunded by Congress with interest in 1842.
1815	May 15	Arrived at Nashville from New Orleans
1817	December 26	Entered upon second Florida campaign.
1818	April 28	Caused the execution of Arbuthnot and Ambrister.
1819	February 8	House of Representatives in Congress sustained Jackson's conduct in the Florida campaign.
1819	Jan. and Feb.	Visited eastern cities.
1819	February	Spain ceded Florida to the United States.
1819		Built Brick Hermitage.
1821		Appointed by President Monroe governor of Florida.
1821	May 31	Resigned from the army.
1821	July 17	Took possession of Florida as governor, and it became a territory of the United States.
1821	October	Resigned as governor of Florida, and returned to Hermitage.
1822	July 20	Nominated for President by the Legislature of Tennessee.
1823		Offered and declined mission to Mexico.
1823	October	Elected to the United States Senate from Tennessee.
1823		Contributed major part of funds for building Presbyterian church in Hermitage neighborhood.
1824	March 4	Nominated for President by the Pennsylvania convention.
1824	November 4	Received plurality of electoral votes for President.
1825	February 9	Defeated for President in the House of Representatives in Congress by John Quincy Adams, who received the vote of thirteen states, Jackson seven, William H. Crawford of Georgia four.
1825		Lafayette visited the Hermitage.
1825	October	Resigned from the United States Senate.
1825	October	Renominated for President by the Legislature of Tennessee.
1826	or 1827	Communion Sunday, date uncertain, promised Mrs. Jackson to join the church when out of politics.
1828	November	Elected President of the United States.
1828	December 22	Death of Mrs. Jackson.
1829	January 17	Left Hermitage for his inauguration.

1829	March 4	Inaugurated President.
1830	April 13	Offered toast: "Our federal union, it must be preserved," at Jefferson's birthday dinner.
1830	December 7	Recommended that the Southern Indians be removed to the Indian Territory.
1831		Two wings added to the Hermitage.
1832	July 10	Vetoed bill re-chartering the Bank of the United States.
1832	November	Re-elected President of the United States.
1832	December 10	Issued proclamation to nullifiers of South Carolina.
1833	June 26	Harvard College conferred the degree of LL.D.
1833	September 23	Ordered withdrawal of deposits from the Bank of the United States.
1834		Hermitage damaged by fire; repaired. No changes since.
1834	March 28	Censured by Senate by resolution for removing public deposits from the Bank of the United States.
1835	December 29	Treaty with the Cherokee Indians for their removal to Indian Territory.
1835	January 8	Proclaimed the payment in full of national debt of the United States.
1837	January 16	Resolution passed in the Senate expunging the resolution of censure of 1834.
1837	March 4	Issued farewell address to people of the United States.
1839		Became a member of the Presbyterian Church near the Hermitage.
1840	January 18	Visited New Orleans.
1845	June 8	Sunday, at 6 P.M., died.
1845	June 10	Buried by the side of Mrs. Jackson at the Hermitage.

OFFICERS AND BOARD OF DIRECTORS
OF
THE LADIES' HERMITAGE ASSOCIATION

Regent..................Mrs. Horatio B. Buntin
First Vice-Regent.......Mrs. Marvin E. Holderness
Second Vice-Regent...............Mrs. Laird Smith
Treasurer.....................Mrs. Roy C. Avery
Recording Secretary............Mrs. Prentice Cooper
Corresponding Secretary.........Miss Martha Lindsey
Mrs. William P. Cooper, *Chairman*, Membership
Miss Marian Craig, *Chairman*, Souvenir Shop
Mrs. John Donelson, *Chairman*, Farm
Mrs. Edward W. Graham, *Chairman*, Garden
Mrs. Ross Greene, *Chairman*, Mansion
Mrs. Douglas Henry, *Chairman*, Restoration, Hermitage
Church
Mrs Marvin E. Holderness, *Chairman*, Museum
Mrs. Fred Russell, *Chairman*, Grounds
Mrs. Joseph S. Reeves, *Chairman*, Program
Mrs. A. MacDowell Smith, *Chairman*, Finance
Mrs. R. D. Stanford, Jr., *Chairman*, Hospitality
Mrs Allen Steele, *Chairman*, Scrapbook
Mrs. William H. Wemyss, *Chairman*, Tulip Grove
Mrs. John Reid Woodward, *Chairman*, Publicity
Mrs. Douglas M. Wright, *Chairman*, Historical Research

Board of Trustees

Mr. Stanley F. Horn, *President*, Nashville
Mr. William Waller, *Vice President*, Nashville
Mr. Henry Barker, Bristol
Mr. Thomas H. Berry, White Pine
Mr. Walter Chandler, Memphis
Mr. Lewis R. Donelson, Jr., Memphis
Mr. J. P. Lawrence, Nashville
Mr. James G. Stahlman, Nashville
Mr. William C. Weaver, Jr., Nashville

MEMBERSHIP OF BOARDS OF THE LHA,
1889 TO PRESENT

ELECTED MAY 15, 1889

Mrs. Mary L. Baxter, Regent
Mrs. A. S. Colyar, First Vice-Regent
Mrs. J. M. Dickinson, 2nd Vice-Regent
Mrs. Mary C. Dorris, Secretary
Mrs. William Morrow
Mrs. John Ruhm
Mrs. Bettie M. Donelson
Mrs. Duncan B. Cooper
Mrs. Felix Demoville
L. F. Benson, Treasurer

•

ELECTED MAY 20, 1891

Mrs. Mary L. Baxter, Regent
Mrs. Albert S. Marks, Acting Regent
Mrs. J. Berrien Lindsley, Sec. Vice-
Regent
Mrs. Mary C. Dorris, Secretary
Mrs. William Morrow
Mrs. John Ruhm
Mrs. Bettie M. Donelson
Mrs. John C. Gaut
Mrs. Maggie L. Hicks
Dr. William Morrow, Treasurer

•

ELECTED JUNE 7, 1893

Mrs. Mary L. Baxter, Regent
Mrs. Albert S. Marks, First Vice-Regent
Mrs. J. Berrien Lindsley, Sec. Vice-
Regent
Mrs. Mary C. Dorris, Secretary
Mrs. John Ruhm, Auditor
Mrs. John C. Gaut
Mrs. Bettie M. Donelson
Mrs. Isabel M. Clark
Mrs. J. M. Dickinson
Mr. Edgar Jones, Treasurer

•

ELECTED OCTOBER 30, 1895

Mrs. Mary L. Baxter, Regent
Mrs. Albert S. Marks, Acting Regent
Mrs. J. Berrien Lindsley, Sec. Vice-
Regent
Mrs. Mary C. Dorris, Secretary
Mrs. John Ruhm, Auditor
Mrs. Hugh Craighead
Mrs. Bettie M. Donelson
Mrs. John C. Gaut
Mrs. Isabel Clark
Mrs. P. H. Manlove, Treasurer

ELECTED MAY 19, 1897

Mrs. Mary L. Baxter, Regent
Mrs. Albert S. Marks, Acting Regent
Mrs. J. Berrien Lindsley, Sec. Vice-
Regent
Mrs. Mary C. Dorris, Secretary
Mrs. R. G. Thorne
Mrs. J. M. Dickinson
Mrs. M. S. Cockrill
Mrs. A. M. Shook
Mrs. John C. Gaut
Mrs. P. H. Manlove, Treasurer

•

ELECTED MAY 17, 1899

Mrs. J. Berrien Lindsley, Regent
Mrs. J. M. Dickinson, First Vice-Regent
Mrs. Eugene C. Lewis, Sec. Vice-Regent
Mrs. Mary C. Dorris, Secretary
Mrs. R. G. Throne
Mrs. M. S. Cockrill
Mrs. A. M. Shook
Mrs. John C. Gaut
Mrs. J. C. Buntin
Mrs. A. M. Shook, Treasurer

•

ELECTED MAY 15, 1901

Mrs. J. Berrien Lindsley, Regent
Mrs. A. M. Shook, First Vice-Regent
Mrs. M. C. Cockrill, Second Vice-Regent
Mrs. Mary C. Dorris, Secretary
Mrs. John C. Gaut
Mrs. William J. McMurray
Mrs. Thomas M. Steger
Mrs. J. C. Buntin
Mrs. J. Walter Allen, Treasurer

•

ELECTED MAY 13, 1903

Mrs. J. Berrien Lindsley, Regent
Mrs. A. M. Shook, First Vice-Regent
Mrs. M. S. Cockrill, Second Vice-Regent
Mrs. Mary C. Dorris, Secretary
Mrs. John C. Gaut
Mrs. William J. McMurray
Mrs. Thomas M. Steger
Mrs. J. C. Buntin
Mrs. J. Walter Allen, Treasurer
   Mrs. Lindsley expiring July 5, 1903.
   Mrs. A. M. Shook was elected Regent,
   Miss Louise Lindsley, a director.

ELECTED MAY 17, 1905

Mrs. Mary C. Dorris, Regent
Mrs. M. S. Cockrill, First Vice-Regent
Miss Louise Lindsley, Second Vice-Regent
Mrs. J. Walter Allen, Secretary
Mrs. William J. McMurray
Mrs. Thomas M. Steger
Mrs. J. C. Buntin
Mrs. A. M. Shook
Mrs. P. H. Manlove, Treasurer

•

ELECTED MAY 15, 1907

Mrs. Mary C. Dorris, Regent
Miss Louise G. Lindsley, First Vice-Regent
Mrs. A. M. Shook, Second Vice-Regent
Mrs. J. Walter Allen, Secretary
Mrs. M. S. Cockrill
Mrs. Thomas M. Steger
Mrs. B. F. Wilson
Mrs. Joseph M. Ford
Mrs. P. H. Manlove, Treasurer

•

ELECTED MAY 19, 1909

Miss Louise Grundy Lindsley, Regent
Mrs. Walter Allen, First Vice-Regent
Mrs. A. M. Shook, Second Vice-Regent
Mrs. Mary C. Dorris, Secretary
Mrs. M. S. Cockrill
Mrs. J. Cleves Symmes
Mrs. B. F. Wilson
Mrs. Joseph M. Ford
Mrs. P. H. Manlove, Treasurer
  Mrs. M. S. Cockrill expired 1910. Mrs. Shelby Williams elected her successor.

•

ELECTED MAY 17, 1911

Miss Louise Grundy Lindsley, Regent
Mrs. J. Walter Allen, First Vice-Regent
Mrs. B. F. Wilson, Second Vice-Regent
Mrs. Mary C. Dorris, Secretary
Mrs. J. Cleves Symmes
Mrs. John C. Brown
Mrs. A. M. Shook
Mrs. James H. Campbell
Mrs. P. H. Manlove, Treasurer

ELECTED MAY 21, 1913

Mrs. B. F. Wilson, Regent
Miss Louise G. Lindsley, First Vice-Regent
Mrs. A. M. Shook, Second Vice-Regent
Mrs. Mary C. Dorris, Secretary
Miss Carrie Sims
Mrs. R. A. Henry
Mrs. Bettie M. Donelson
Mrs. Maggie L. Hicks
Mrs. P. H. Manlove, Treasurer

•

ELECTED MAY 19, 1915

Mrs. B. F. Wilson, Regent
Miss Louise G. Lindsley, First Vice-Regent
Mrs. A. M. Shook, Second Vice-Regent
Mrs. Mary C. Dorris, Secretary
Miss Carrie Sims
Mrs. R. A. Henry
Mrs. Bettie M. Donelson
Mrs. Maggie L. Hicks
Mrs. P. H. Manlove, Treasurer
  Mrs. P. H. Manlove expiring February 27, 1917. Mrs. Maggie L. Hicks was elected treasurer and Mrs. Porter Phillips a director.

•

ELECTED MAY 16, 1917

Mrs. Bettie M. Donelson, Regent
Mrs. B. F. Wilson, First Vice-Regent
Miss Louise G. Lindsley, Sec. Vice-Regent
Mrs. Maggie L. Hicks, Treasurer
Mrs. Mary C. Dorris, Secretary
Mrs. A. M. Shook
Mrs. Porter Phillips
Mrs. R. A. Henry
Mrs. J. Washington Moore

•

ELECTED MAY 21, 1919

Mrs. Bettie M. Donelson, Regent
Mrs. B. F. Wilson, First Vice-Regent
Miss Louise G. Lindsley, Sec. Vice-Regent
Mrs. Maggie L. Hicks, Treasurer
Mrs. Mary C. Dorris, Secretary
Mrs. E. T. Lowe
Mrs. Porter Phillips
Mrs. Harry Evans
Mrs. R. A. Henry

ELECTED MAY 18, 1921

Mrs. Harry Evans, Regent
Mrs. Alex Caldwell, First Vice-Regent
Mrs. James S. Frazer, Second Vice-Regent
Mrs. Mary C. Dorris, Secretary
Mrs. Maggie L. Hicks, Treasurer
Miss Louise G. Lindsley
Mrs. R. A. Henry
Mrs. Joseph H. Thompson
Mrs. Walter Stokes
   Mrs. Harry Evans resigned April 4th, 1922.
   Mrs. Henry elected Regent and Mrs. McFarland a director. Mrs. Maggie L. Hicks resigned December, 1921. Mrs. E. A. Lindsey elected treasurer. Mrs. Joseph H. Thompson resigned and Mrs. Reau Folk elected October, 1921.

•

ELECTED MAY 1922

Mrs. R. A. Henry, Regent
Mrs. Alex Caldwell, First Vice-Regent
Mrs. James S. Frazer, Second Vice-Regent
Mrs. Mary C. Dorris, Secretary
Mrs. Maggie L. Hicks, Treasurer
Miss Louise G. Lindsley
Mrs. Reau Folk
Mrs. Walter Stokes
Mrs. Craig McFarland

•

ELECTED MAY 16, 1923

Mrs. Walter Stokes, Regent
Mrs. Alex Caldwell, First Vice-Regent
Mrs. James S. Frazer, Sec. Vice-Regent
Mrs. Mary C. Dorris, Secretary
Mrs. E. A. Lindsey, Treasurer
Miss Louise G. Lindsley
Mrs. Reau Folk
Mrs. Craig McFarland
Mrs. John T. Henderson

•

ELECTED MAY 20, 1925

Mrs. Walter Stokes, Regent
Mrs. James Frazer, First Vice-Regent
Mrs. E. W. Graham, Second Vice-Regent
Mrs. Reau Folk, Secretary
Mrs. E. A. Lindsey, Treasurer
Miss Louise G. Lindsley
Mrs. Craig McFarland
Mrs. H. L. Sperry
Mrs. J. M. Overton

ELECTED MAY 18, 1927

Mrs. James S. Frazer, Regent
Mrs. Edward A. Lindsey, 1st Vice-Regent
Mrs. E. W. Graham, Second Vice-Regent
Mrs. Reau E. Folk, Secretary
Mrs. Lyon Childress, Treasurer
Miss Louise G. Lindsley
Mrs. H. L. Sperry
Mrs. Jesse M. Overton
Mrs. James E. Caldwell, Sr.

•

ELECTED MAY 15, 1929

Mrs. Edward A. Lindsey, Regent
Mrs. Reau E. Folk, First Vice-Regent
Mrs. E. W. Graham, Second Vice-Regent
Mrs. H. L. Sperry, Secretary
Mrs. Lyon Childress, Treasurer
Miss Louise G. Lindsley
Mrs. Jesse M. Overton
Mrs. James E. Caldwell
Mrs. Edgar M. Foster

•

ELECTED MAY 20, 1931

Mrs. Edward A. Lindsey, Regent
Mrs. Reau E. Folk, First Vice-Regent
Mrs. E. W. Graham, Second Vice-Regent
Mrs. Lyon Childress, Treasurer
Mrs. Paul DeWitt, Secretary
Miss Louise G. Lindsley
Mrs. Jesse M. Overton
Mrs. James E. Caldwell
Mrs. Edgar M. Foster

•

ELECTED MAY 17, 1933

Mrs. Reau E. Folk, Regent
Mrs. E. W. Graham, First Vice-Regent
Mrs. James E. Caldwell, Sec. Vice-Regent
Mrs. Paul DeWitt, Recording Secretary
Mrs. Walter Stokes, Corresponding Sec.
Mrs. Lyon Childress, Treasurer
Miss Louise G. Lindsley
Mrs. E. A. Lindsey
Mrs. Jesse M. Overton
Mrs. Edgar M. Foster
Mrs. George Blackie

ELECTED MAY, 1935

Mrs. Reau E. Folk, Regent
Mrs. E. W. Graham, First Vice-Regent
Mrs. James E. Caldwell, Sec. Vice-Regent
Mrs. Paul DeWitt, Recording Secretary
Mrs. Walter Stokes, Corresponding Sec.
Mrs. Lyon Childress, Treasurer
Miss Louise G. Lindsley
Mrs. E. A. Lindsey
Mrs. Jesse M. Overton
Mrs. Edgar M. Foster
Mrs. George Blackie

•

ELECTED MAY, 1937

Mrs. Jesse M. Overton, Regent
Mrs. E. W. Graham, First Vice-Regent
Mrs. James E. Caldwell, Sec. Vice-Regent
Mrs. Paul DeWitt, Recording Secretary
Mrs. Walter Stokes, Corresponding Sec.
Mrs. Lyon Childress, Treasurer
Miss Louise G. Lindsley
Mrs. E. A. Lindsey
Mrs. Edgar M. Foster
Mrs. George Blackie
Mrs. Reau E. Folk

•

ELECTED MAY, 1939

Mrs. Jesse M. Overton, Regent
Mrs. E. W. Graham, First Vice-Regent
Mrs. James E. Caldwell, Sec. Vice-Regent
Mrs. Paul DeWitt, Recording Secretary
Mrs. Geo. Blackie, Corresponding Secretary
Mrs. Lyon Childress, Treasurer
Miss Louise G. Lindsley
Mrs. Charles Buntin
Mrs. Edgar M. Foster
Mrs. Walter Stokes
   Mrs. James E. Caldwell expired 1939, and Mrs. Edgar Foster was elected her successor.
   Miss Martha Lindsey was elected to the Board.

•

ELECTED MAY, 1941

Mrs. Edward W. Graham, Regent
Mrs. Edgar M. Foster, First Vice-Regent
Mrs. George F. Blackie, Sec. Vice-Regent
Mrs. Lyon Childress, Treasurer
Mrs. Paul DeWitt, Recording Secretary
Miss Martha Lindsey, Cor. Secretary
Mrs. Walter Stokes
Mrs. Charles E. Buntin
Mrs. Jesse M. Overton
Miss Louise G. Lindsley

ELECTED MAY, 1943

Mrs. Edward W. Graham, Regent
Mrs. Edgar M. Foster, First Vice-Regent
Mrs. George F. Blackie, Sec. Vice-Regent
Mrs. Lyon Childress, Treasurer
Mrs. Paul DeWitt, Recording Secretary
Miss Martha Lindsey, Cor. Secretary
Mrs. Walter Stokes
Mrs. Charles E. Buntin
Miss Louise G. Lindsley
Mrs. Douglas M. Wright
Mrs. Robert F. Jackson, Sr.

•

ELECTED MAY, 1945

Mrs. George F. Blackie, Regent
Mrs. Edgar M. Foster, First Vice-Regent
Mrs. Robert F. Jackson, Sec. Vice-Regent
Mrs. Lyon Childress, Treasurer
Miss Martha Lindsey, Recording Secretary
Mrs. Douglas M. Wright, Cor. Secretary
Mrs. Walter Stokes
Mrs. Paul DeWitt
Mrs. Chas. E. Buntin
Mrs. E. W. Graham
Mrs. Jesse M. Overton
Miss Fermine Pride
Mrs. William P. Cooper
Mrs. Roy Avery

•

ELECTED MAY, 1947

Mrs. George F. Blackie, Regent
Mrs. Edgar M. Foster, First Vice-Regent
Mrs. Robert F. Jackson, Sec. Vice-Regent
Mrs. Lyon Childress, Treasurer
Miss Martha Lindsey, Recording Secretary
Mrs. Douglas M. Wright, Cor. Secretary
Mrs. Walter Stokes
Mrs. Paul DeWitt
Mrs. Chas. E. Buntin
Mrs. E. W. Graham
Mrs. Jesse M. Overton
Miss Fermine Pride
Mrs. William P. Cooper
Mrs. Roy Avery

ELECTED MAY, 1949

Mrs. Robert F. Jackson, Regent
Mrs. William P. Cooper, First Vice-
Regent
Miss Fermine Pride, Second Vice-Regent
Mrs. Roy Avery, Treasurer
Miss Martha Lindsey, Recording Sec-
retary
Mrs. Douglas M. Wright, Cor. Secretary
Mrs. George F. Blackie
Mrs. Charles E. Buntin
Mrs. Lyon Childress
Mrs. Paul DeWitt
Mrs. Edgar M. Foster
Mrs. E. W. Graham
Mrs. Douglas Henry
Mrs. Gilbert S. Merritt
Mrs. Jesse M. Overton
Mrs. William H. Wemyss

•

ELECTED MAY, 1951

Mrs. W. H. Wemyss, Regent
Mrs. William P. Cooper, First Vice-
Regent
Miss Fermine Pride, Second Vice-Regent
Mrs. Roy C. Avery, Treasurer
Miss Martha Lindsey, Recording Sec-
retary
Mrs. Douglas M. Wright, Cor. Secretary
Mrs. George F. Blackie
Mrs. Charles Buntin
Mrs. Lyon Childress
Mrs. Paul E. DeWitt
Mrs. Edgar M. Foster
Mrs. E. W. Graham
Mrs. Douglas Henry
Mrs. Robert F. Jackson
Mrs. Gilbert S. Merritt
Mrs. Jesse M. Overton

•

ELECTED MAY, 1953

Mrs. W. H. Wemyss, Regent
Mrs. William P. Cooper, First Vice-
Regent
Miss Fermine Pride, Second Vice-Regent
Mrs. Roy C. Avery, Treasurer
Miss Martha Lindsey, Recording Sec-
retary
Mrs. Douglas M. Wright, Cor. Secretary
Mrs. George F. Blackie
Mrs. Charles Buntin
Mrs. Lyon Childress

Mrs. Paul E. DeWitt
Mrs. Edgar M. Foster
Mrs. E. W. Graham
Mrs. Douglas Henry
Mrs. Robert F. Jackson
Mrs. Gilbert S. Merritt
Mrs. Jesse M. Overton
Mrs. A. MacDowell Smith

•

ELECTED MAY, 1955

Mrs. Douglas Henry, Regent
Mrs. William P. Cooper, First Vice-
Regent
Miss Fermine Pride, Second Vice-Regent
Mrs. Roy C. Avery, Treasurer
Miss Martha Lindsey, Recording Sec-
retary
Mrs. Douglas M. Wright, Corres. Sec-
retary
Mrs. Geo. F. Blackie
Mrs. Horatio B. Buntin
Mrs. Lyon Childress
Mrs. Paul E. DeWitt
Mrs. Edgar M. Foster
Mrs. E. W. Graham
Mrs. Henry Goodpasture
Mrs. Robert F. Jackson
Mrs. Gilbert S. Merritt
Mrs. Jesse M. Overton
Mrs. A. MacDowell Smith
Mrs. William H. Wemyss

•

ELECTED MAY, 1957

Mrs. William P. Cooper, Regent
Miss Martha Lindsey, First Vice-Regent
Miss Fermine Pride, Second Vice-Regent
Mrs. Roy C. Avery, Treasurer
Mrs. Horatio B. Buntin, Secretary
Mrs. Douglas M. Wright, Corres. Sec-
retary
Mrs. George F. Blackie
Mrs. Paul E. DeWitt
Mrs. Edgar M. Foster
Mrs. Henry Goodpasture
Mrs. E. W. Graham
Mrs. Douglas Henry
Mrs. Robert F. Jackson
Mrs. Gilbert S. Merritt
Mrs. Jesse M. Overton
Mrs. A. MacDowell Smith
Mrs. William H. Wemyss

ELECTED MAY, 1959

Miss Martha Lindsey, Regent
Mrs. Douglas S. Henry, First Vice-Regent
Mrs. E. W. Graham, Second Vice-Regent
Mrs. Roy C. Avery, Treasurer
Mrs. Horatio B. Buntin, Secretary
Mrs. Douglas M. Wright, Corres. Secretary
Mrs. George F. Blackie
Mrs. William P. Cooper
Mrs. Paul E. DeWitt
Mrs. Edgar M. Foster
Mrs. Henry Goodpasture
Mrs. Gilbert S. Merritt
Mrs. Jesse M. Overton
Mrs. A. McDowell Smith
Mrs. William H. Wemyss
Mrs. John Reid Woodward

•

ELECTED MAY, 1961

Mrs. A. MacDowell Smith, Regent
Mrs. William P. Cooper, First Vice-Regent
Mrs. E. W. Graham, Second Vice-Regent
Mrs. Roy C. Avery, Treasurer
Mrs. Horatio Buntin, Recording Secretary
Mrs. Douglas M. Wright, Corresponding Secretary
Mrs. George F. Blackie
Miss Marian Craig
Mrs. Paul E. DeWitt
Mrs. Edgar M. Foster
Mrs. Henry Goodpasture
Mrs. Douglas Henry
Mrs. Marvin E. Holderness
Miss Martha Lindsey
Mrs. Gilbert S. Merritt
Mrs. Jesse M. Overton
Mrs. Fred Russell
Mrs. Laird Smith
Mrs. William H. Wemyss
Mrs. John Reid Woodward

•

ELECTED MAY, 1963

Mrs. A. MacDowell Smith, Regent
Mrs. William P. Cooper, First Vice-Regent
Mrs. E. W. Graham, Second Vice-Regent
Mrs. Roy C. Avery, Treasurer
Mrs. Horatio Buntin, Recording Secretary
Miss Martha Lindsey, Corresponding Secretary
Mrs. George M. Blackie
Miss Marian Craig
Mrs. Paul E. DeWitt
Mrs. Edgar M. Foster
Mrs. Henry Goodpasture
Mrs. Douglas Henry
Mrs. Marvin E. Holderness

Mrs. Gilbert S. Merritt
Mrs. Jesse M. Overton
Mrs. Fred Russell
Mrs. Laird Smith
Mrs. William H. Wemyss
Mrs. John Reid Woodward
Mrs. Douglas M. Wright

•

ELECTED MAY, 1965

Mrs. Horatio B. Buntin, Regent
Mrs. William P. Cooper, First Vice-Regent
Mrs. Edward W. Graham, Second Vice-Regent
Mrs. Roy C. Avery, Treasurer
Mrs. Laird Smith, Recording Secretary
Miss Martha Lindsey, Corresponding Secretary
Mrs. George F. Blackie
Miss Marian Craig
Mrs. Paul E. DeWitt
Mrs. Edgar M. Foster
Mrs. Ross Greene
Mrs. Douglas Henry
Mrs. Marvin E. Holderness
Mrs. Gilbert Merritt
Mrs. Fred Russell
Mrs. Joseph Sl Reeves
Mrs. A. MacDowell Smith
Mrs. R. D. Stanford, Jr.
Mrs. William H. Wemyss
Mrs. John Reid Woodward
Mrs. Douglas M. Wright

•

ELECTED MAY, 1967

Mrs. Horatio Buntin, Regent
Mrs. Marvin E. Holderness, First Vice-Regent
Mrs. Laird Smith, Second Vice-Regent
Mrs. Roy C. Avery, Treasurer
Mrs. Prentice Cooper, Recording Secretary
Miss Martha Lindsey, Corresponding Secretary
Mus. William P. Cooper
Miss Marian Craig
Mrs. Paul Dewitt
Mrs. John Donelson
Mrs. Edward W. Graham
Mrs. Ross Greene
Mrs. Douglas Henry
Mrs. Fred Russell
Mrs. Joseph S. Reeves
Mrs. Allen Steele (elected June, 1967)
Mrs. A. MacDowell Smith
Mrs. R. D. Stanford
Mrs. William H. Wemyss
Mrs. John Reid Woodward
Mrs. Douglas M. Wright

BOOKS AND PAMPHLETS WRITTEN ABOUT ANDREW JACKSON

PUBLICATIONS IN TENNESSEE STATE LIBRARY AND ARCHIVES

Author	Title	Date of Publication
Jackson, Andrew	Correspondence, 7 vols., ed. by John S. Bassett	1926–35
An American Officer	Civil and Military History of Andrew Jackson	1825
Bassett, John S.	The Life of Andrew Jackson, 2 vols.	1911
Bowers, Claude G.	Party Battles of the Jackson Period	1922
Brady, Cyrus T.	The True Andrew Jackson	1906
Brown, William G.	Andrew Jackson	1900
Augustus G. Buell	History of Andrew Jackson	1904
Campbell, Tom W.	Two Fighters and Two Fines	1941
Citizen of New York	Memoirs of General Andrew Jackson	1845
Cobbett, William	Life of Andrew Jackson	1834
Colyar, Arthur St. C.	Life and Times of Andrew Jackson	1904
Dusenbery, Ben M.	Monument to the Memory of Gen. Jackson	1845
Eaton, John H.	The Life of Andrew Jackson	1817
Frost, John	Pictorial Life of Andrew Jackson	1847
Gentleman of the Baltimore Bar	Some Account of Gen. Jackson	1828
Goodwin, Philo A.	Biography of Andrew Jackson	1832
Headley, Joel T.	The Life of Andrew Jackson	1880
Heiskell, Saml. G.	Andrew Jackson and Early Tenn. History, 3 vols.	1920
James, Marquis	Andrew Jackson, 2 vols.	1938
Jenkins, Jno. S.	Life and Public Services of Gen. Andrew Jackson	1880
Johnson, Gerald W.	Andrew Jackson, An Epic in Homespun	1927
Karsner, David	Andrew Jackson, The Gentle Savage	1929
Macdonald, Wm.	Jacksonian Democracy, 1829–1837	1906
Mayo, Robert	Political Sketches of Eight Years in Washington	1839
Nicolay, Helen	Andrew Jackson, The Fighting President	1929
Ogg, Frederic A.	The Reign of Andrew Jackson	1921
Parton, James	Life of Andrew Jackson, 2 vols.	1860
Peck, Charles H.	The Jacksonian Epoch	1899
Rowland, Eron O.	Andrew Jackson's Campaign Against the British	1926
Schlesinger, Arthur M.	The Age of Jackson	1945
Snelling, William J.	A Brief, Impartial History by a Free Man	1831
Sumner, William G.	Andrew Jackson	1910
Syrett, Harold G.	Andrew Jackson, His Contibution	1953
Van Deusen, Glyndon	The Jacksonian Era, 1828-1848	1959
Waldo, Samuel P.	Memoirs of Andrew Jackson	1819

Walker, Alexander..........Jackson and New Orleans......................1856
Ward, John W.............Andrew Jackson, Symbol for an Age............1955

FOR YOUNG READERS

Coy, Harold...............Real Book About Andrew Jackson..............1952
James, Bessie R............The Courageous Heart.........................1934
Judson, Clara I............Andrew Jackson..............................1954

In addition to the above, the State Library has many valuable, rare, and out-of-print pamphlets on General Jackson.

Microfilms of Hermitage Letters and Documents are available at Joint University Library

PUBLICATIONS SOLD BY THE LHA

The Hermitage, A History and Guide (Catalogue, Historiacl Data, Pictures)..35c

The Hermitage, Home of Old Hickory........STANLEY F. HORN $3.95

Andrew Jackson's Hermitage.........MARY FRENCH CALDWELL $1.50

The Battle of New Orleans, Its Real Meaning.......REAU E. FOLK 35c

MR. BANCROFT'S ORATION ON THE DEATH OF ANDREW JACKSON..25c

Preservation of the Hermitage...........MRS. MARY C. DORRIS $2.00

Rachel Jackson.......................MRS. WALTER STOKES 35c

Advice to Jackson from His Mother...........................25c

Andrew Jackson, Man of Destiny............WILLIAM E. BEARD 10c

President's Lady...........................IRVING STONE $4.95

The Hermitage...........................STANLEY F. HORN 50c

Constitution of the United States, Declaration of Independence Historical Facts and Data.................................30c

Historic Documents; Declaration of Independence, Constitution of United States, Bill of Rights, Lincoln's Gettysburg Address.........$1.00

Andrew Jackson and Freemasonry,.............PAUL E. DeWITT 35c
Various Postcards and Slides

Tulip Grove.......................STEPHEN S. LAWRENCE 50c

Portrait of a President...................MARQUIS JAMES $2.50

The Border Captain......................MARQUIS JAMES $1.95

Autobiography of Emily Donelson Walton.....................$1.00

Landmarks of Tennessee History
...................EDITED BY ALDERSON AND McBRIDE $4.00

White Pillars...........................J. FRAZER SMITH $3.50

American Homes in History.............Arnold Nicholson $12.95

First Ladies Cook Book....................................$7.75

Santa Claus at the White House in Old Hickory's Day............35c

Tennessee at the Battle of New Orleans..........Elbert Watson 50c

FOR YOUNG READERS

Andrew Jackson........................Genevieve Foster $3.25

Rachel Jackson, Tennessee Girl.......Christine Noble Govan $2.25

The Jacksons of Tennessee................Marguerite Vance $3.75

Andrew Jackson, The Fighting Frontiersman
..........................Frances Fitzpatrick Wright $1.75

Andrew Jackson, Frontier Statesman.....Clara Ingram Judson $3.75

Historic Sites in Tennessee.....Tennessee Historical Commission 50c

Tennessee Historical Markers...Tennessee Historical Commissirn 75c

The White House, A Historical Guide, regular edition
....................White House Historical Association $1.25

The Presidents of the U. S. A. regular edition
.....................White House Historical Association 75c

THE HERMITAGE
HOME OF ANDREW JACKSON

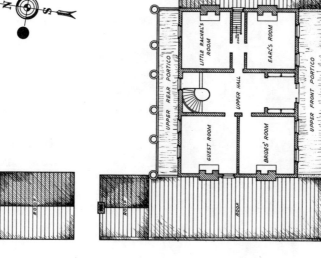

SECOND FLOOR PLAN

DRAWN BY BOB HOLLINGSWORTH
JUNE 27, 1967

FIRST FLOOR PLAN

THE HERMITAGE

HOME OF ANDREW JACKSON

A PERSPECTIVE VIEW

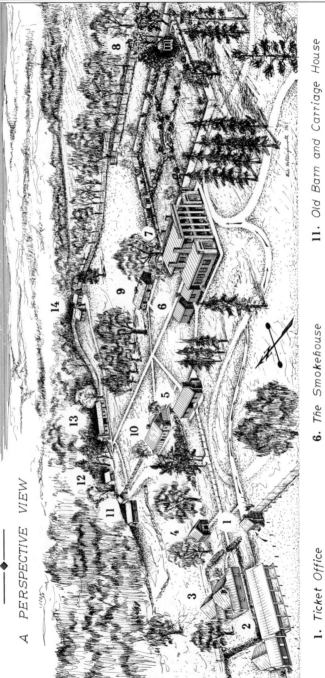

1. Ticket Office
2. Gift Shop
3. Custodian's Home
4. The Carriage House
5. The Museum
6. The Smokehouse
7. The Mansion
8. The Tomb
9. Uncle Alfred's Cabin
10. Farm Shop and Greenhouse
11. Old Barn and Carriage House from Hunter's Hill
12. Stone Spring House
13. Cabin by the Spring
14. The Early Hermitage